THE TIME ALCHEMIST

MASTERING TIME MANAGEMENT FOR PEAK PERFORMANCE

DR. MINAKSHI BANSAL

DEDICATION

To all those who dare to seize the reins of time and transform their lives.

♥♥♥

Contents

Contents

Prayer

"Om Bhadram Karnebhih Shrinuyama Devah

Bhadram Pashyemakshabhiryajatrah

Sthirairangais Tushtuvamsastanubhih

Vyashema Devahitam Yadayuh

Svasti Na Indro Vriddhashravah

Svasti Nah Pusha Vishwavedah

Svasti Nastarkshyo Arishtanemih

Svasti No Brihaspatir Dadhatu

Om Shantih Shantih Shantih"

This mantra is a prayer for universal well-being, invoking the blessings of various deities for protection, health, and happiness. It emphasizes the importance of experiencing the auspicious through all senses and living a life aligned with divine purpose. The repetition of "Shantih" at the end signifies a deep desire for peace in the individual, the environment, and the universe at large. This mantra is often recited as a prayer for peace, prosperity, and the physical and spiritual well-being of all beings.

ᐅᐅᐅ

About The Author

This book represents the culmination of extensive research and meticulous analysis, incorporating a diverse range of sources, including numerous books, scholarly studies, and personal experiences. Additionally, I have scoured various websites to gather relevant information and data essential for the compilation of this work. I have taken every precaution to ensure the accuracy of the information presented and have diligently cited all sources to acknowledge their contributions.

From her earliest days, Minakshi was distinguished by an insatiable appetite for reading. Her literary universe was inhabited by characters and narratives that spanned ethical tales, motivational and inspirational stories, and the mythic parables imbued with life lessons. This voracious reading habit was not merely for personal edification but was driven by a desire to distill and disseminate the essence of these narratives to foster the development of students and peers alike. She was particularly captivated by the lives and teachings of historical figures and spiritual leaders such as Adi Shankaracharya, Swami Vivekananda, Dr. APJ Abdul Kalam, Mahamana Pandit Madan Mohan Malviya, Mahatma Gandhi, Sardar Vallabhai Patel, and Vinoba Bhave, among others. Their philosophies and life stories fueled her ambition to embody their ideals of resilience, selflessness, and relentless pursuit of knowledge.

Dr. Minakshi's academic and practical engagement with psychology has been equally noteworthy. As a research scholar, her focus has been on exploring the intricate tapestry of the human psyche, aiming to unlock the potential for psychological well-being and societal harmony. Her scholarly work is complemented by her active involvement in social work, where she employs her academic insights to make tangible differences in the lives of the underprivileged. Her endeavours in social work are characterized by an innovative approach that combines traditional wisdom with contemporary psychological practices to address the multifaceted challenges faced by these communities.

Her artistic talents, another facet of her diverse capabilities, are not merely a personal passion but also serve as a medium through which she communicates and connects with others. Her art, rich in symbolism and emotional depth, reflects her philosophical inquiries and social concerns, offering viewers a glimpse into the breadth of her intellect and the depth of her compassion.

In addition to her contributions to the arts and social sciences, Dr. Minakshi has embraced the healing arts of Pranic Healing, mastering the techniques developed by Master Choa Kok Sui. This practice, which focuses on the manipulation of Prana or life energy to heal the body and aura, has been both a personal journey of discovery and a means through which she extends her healing touch to others. Her proficiency in Pranic Healing is complemented by her advocacy and teaching of various forms of meditation aimed at rejuvenation, personal betterment, and the cultivation of harmony within individuals and communities alike.

Dr. Minakshi's life is a narrative of relentless pursuit, not just of personal achievement but of the upliftment and empowerment of society at large. Her diverse interests and talents—spanning the arts, literature, psychology, and the healing practices—converge on a singular path of service. She embodies the spirit of the luminaries who inspired her, channelling their legacy through her actions and teachings. Through her books, art, and social initiatives, she continues to inspire a new generation to embark on their own journeys of self-discovery, resilience, and altruism.

Her commitment to social betterment, particularly her focus on uplifting underprivileged children, reflects a deep understanding of the transformative potential of education and personal development. By integrating her knowledge of psychology, her artistic sensibilities, and her healing practices, Dr. Bansal has developed a holistic approach to social work that addresses both the immediate needs and the long-term well-being of the communities she serves.

As an author, Dr. Minakshi's writings offer a blend of inspirational insights, practical wisdom, and reflective contemplations drawn from her extensive reading and life experiences. Her books serve as a guide for those seeking to navigate the complexities of life with grace, resilience, and purpose. Through her narratives, she extends an invitation to her readers to explore the depths of their own potential and to contribute meaningfully to the collective well-being of society.

In Dr. Minakshi Bansal, we find a remarkable synthesis of the artist, the scholar, the healer, and the social activist. Her life's work stands as a beacon of hope and a source of inspiration for individuals seeking to make a difference in the world. Her story is a compelling reminder of the power of individual action, rooted in compassion and driven by a profound commitment to the betterment of humanity. Dr. Minakshi's legacy is not just in the tangible outcomes of her efforts but in the enduring spirit of inquiry, empathy, and service that she embodies.

ﯨﯨﯨ

Preface

In the tapestry of life, time is the most precious thread we possess. It weaves together our moments, days, and years, shaping our experiences, defining our accomplishments, and ultimately determining the legacy we leave behind. Yet, time is also the most elusive and fleeting of resources, constantly slipping through our fingers like grains of sand. In our relentless pursuit of success, happiness, and fulfillment, we often find ourselves wrestling with the constraints of time, struggling to balance competing demands, and yearning for a greater sense of control over our lives.

It is within this universal struggle that the seeds of this book were sown. Over the years, I have had the privilege of guiding countless individuals on their journeys toward mastering time management. I have witnessed firsthand the transformative power of time alchemy, the art of turning the ordinary into the extraordinary by harnessing the power of the present moment and aligning our actions with our deepest intentions. I have seen individuals from all walks of life overcome seemingly insurmountable obstacles, achieve remarkable feats, and create lives of profound meaning and purpose, all by mastering the art of time management.

Inspired by these transformative journeys, I embarked on a quest to distill the essence of time alchemy into a comprehensive guide that could empower others to reclaim their time, unleash their potential, and live lives of greater fulfillment. This book is the culmination of that quest, a distillation of years of experience, research, and reflection on the art and science of time management.

Within these pages, you will find a wealth of practical strategies, tools, and techniques for mastering time management. You will learn how to set clear and compelling goals, prioritize your tasks, overcome procrastination, and create a personalized time blueprint that aligns with your values and aspirations. You will also discover the power of mindfulness, energy management, delegation, and the 80/20 Rule in maximizing your productivity and achieving your goals.

But this book is more than just a collection of practical tips and tricks. It is a journey of self-discovery, a exploration of the deeper meaning and purpose of time. Through the pages of this book, I invite you to embark on a journey of self-reflection, to explore your own relationship with time, and to discover the unique rhythms and patterns that shape your life.

As you delve into the concepts and practices presented in this book, you will come to realize that time management is not about rigidly controlling your schedule or squeezing every last drop of productivity from your day. Rather, it is about aligning your actions with your intentions, living in the present moment, and creating a life that is both meaningful and fulfilling. It is about embracing the power of choice, recognizing that you are the architect of your own destiny, and choosing to spend your time in ways that nourish your soul and propel you towards your goals.

The journey towards mastering time management is not always easy. It requires discipline, commitment, and a willingness to confront our own limitations and fears. But the rewards are immeasurable. By mastering the art of time alchemy, we can break free from the shackles of overwhelm, reclaim control of our lives, and create a legacy that will endure long after we are gone.

Whether you are a student struggling to balance your studies with your social life, a professional juggling multiple deadlines and responsibilities, or an entrepreneur striving to build a successful business, the principles and practices outlined in this book can help you to achieve your goals, maximize your productivity, and create a life that is both meaningful and fulfilling.

I invite you to embrace the journey that lies ahead, to experiment with the various techniques and strategies presented in this book, and to discover your own unique path to time mastery. Remember, the power to transform your life lies within you. It is simply a matter of harnessing the power of the present moment, aligning your actions with your intentions, and embracing the endless possibilities that time has to offer.

May this book serve as your guide and companion on this transformative journey. May it inspire you to reclaim your time, unleash your potential, and create a life that is truly extraordinary.

Dr. Minakshi Bansal
Social Activist
Ahmedabad, Gujarat, Bharat

ppp

ONE

THE TIME ILLUSION: UNMASKING THE MYTH OF SCARCITY

Time, the elusive phantom, ceaselessly marches forward, shaping our lives, defining our experiences, and yet, it remains one of the most misunderstood concepts in human existence. We perceive it as a finite resource, a scarce commodity that must be meticulously rationed and guarded against depletion. This perception, however, is a deceptive illusion, a misconception that has been deeply ingrained in our collective consciousness.

The illusion of time scarcity is not a recent phenomenon. It has been woven into the fabric of our societal narratives, perpetuated by cultural norms, and reinforced by the relentless pace of modern life. We are bombarded with messages that emphasize the urgency of time, the need to maximize productivity, and the fear of missing out. This creates a constant sense of pressure, a feeling that we are perpetually running out of time.

The roots of this illusion can be traced back to our evolutionary past. In the harsh environments our ancestors inhabited, time was indeed a precious resource. Food had to be gathered, shelter had to be built, and threats had to be avoided, all within the constraints of the day-night cycle. This survival imperative instilled in us a deep-seated fear of scarcity, a fear that has persisted even as our circumstances have drastically changed.

In the modern world, we no longer face the same existential threats as our ancestors. We have developed technologies that have dramatically increased our life expectancy, improved our living standards, and provided us with unprecedented access to information and resources. Yet, the illusion of time scarcity persists, fueled by a relentless pursuit of material wealth, social status, and personal achievement.

The illusion of time scarcity is not merely a harmless misconception. It has profound implications for our well-being, our relationships, and our overall quality of life. When we believe that time is scarce, we become anxious, stressed, and overwhelmed. We prioritize immediate gratification over long-term goals, and we sacrifice meaningful experiences for the sake of fleeting pleasures.

Furthermore, the illusion of time scarcity perpetuates a culture of overwork, burnout, and dissatisfaction. We feel compelled to constantly do more, achieve more, and be more, even at the expense of our health, our happiness, and our relationships. This relentless pursuit of productivity creates a vicious cycle, where we work harder to gain more time, only to find that we have less time to enjoy the fruits of our labor.

To break free from the illusion of time scarcity, we must first challenge the underlying assumptions that perpetuate it. We must recognize that time is not a finite resource, but rather a subjective experience that is shaped by our perceptions, our priorities, and our choices.

One of the key factors that contribute to the illusion of time scarcity is our tendency to focus on the past and the future, rather than the present moment. When we dwell on past regrets or future anxieties, we lose sight of the only time that truly matters: the here and now. By cultivating mindfulness, we can learn to fully inhabit the present moment, savoring each experience and appreciating the richness of our lives.

Another factor that perpetuates the illusion of time scarcity is our tendency to overcommit and overschedule. We fill our calendars with meetings, appointments, and obligations, leaving little time for rest, relaxation, and spontaneity. By learning to say no to unnecessary commitments and prioritizing activities that align with our values and goals, we can reclaim our time and create space for the things that truly matter.

Finally, we must challenge the societal narratives that reinforce the illusion of time scarcity. We must reject the notion that our worth is determined by our productivity, our achievements, or our material possessions. We must embrace a more holistic view of success, one that encompasses well-being, relationships, and personal fulfillment.

By unmasking the myth of time scarcity, we can unlock the true potential of our lives. We can cultivate a deeper sense of purpose, meaning, and joy. We can build stronger relationships, pursue our passions, and make a positive impact on the world. And we can learn to appreciate the precious gift of time, not as a scarce commodity to be hoarded, but as a boundless resource to be cherished and shared.

ᎭᎭᎭ

*Time is not your enemy, but your greatest ally.
Embrace its flow, harness its power, and create a
life that is both meaningful and fulfilling.
Remember, the present moment is the only time you
truly have.*

TWO
TIME ALCHEMY 101. THE FUNDAMENTALS OF TIME TRANSFORMATION

Time, often perceived as a relentless, linear force, can feel like an insurmountable adversary. We strive to bend it to our will, to squeeze every last drop of productivity from its fleeting moments. Yet, the pursuit of mastering time often leaves us feeling overwhelmed and defeated. What if, instead of trying to control time, we could transform it? This is the essence of Time Alchemy 101, the fundamental principles that empower us to shift our relationship with time from one of scarcity and stress to one of abundance and flow.

At its core, Time Alchemy is not about manipulating the clock or bending the laws of physics. It is about shifting our perception of time, recognizing its inherent flexibility, and harnessing its transformative power. Just as alchemists of old sought to transmute base metals into gold, we can transmute our relationship with time into a source of empowerment and fulfillment.

The first principle of Time Alchemy is awareness. We must become acutely aware of how we currently spend our time, the habits that govern our days, and the underlying beliefs that shape our perception of time. This awareness can be cultivated through the practice of time tracking, where we meticulously record how we allocate our hours and minutes. This simple act of observation can reveal surprising insights into our time usage patterns, highlighting areas where we may be unconsciously squandering our most precious resource.

Once we have developed a heightened awareness of our time usage, we can begin to identify the time leaks that drain our energy and productivity. These leaks can take many forms, from mindless scrolling through social media to attending unproductive meetings to engaging in activities that do not align with our values and goals. By plugging these leaks, we reclaim valuable time that can be redirected towards more meaningful pursuits.

The second principle of Time Alchemy is intentionality. We must approach each moment with a clear sense of purpose and intention, choosing how we want to spend our time rather than allowing it to be dictated by external forces or ingrained habits. This requires us to develop a strong internal compass, a set of values and priorities that guide our decisions and actions. By aligning our time usage with our deepest values, we infuse our days with meaning and purpose.

Intentionality also involves setting clear goals and objectives for how we want to use our time. These goals can be short-term, such as completing a specific task, or long-term, such as achieving a major life milestone. By setting clear goals, we create a roadmap for our time, ensuring that our actions are aligned with our desired outcomes.

The third principle of Time Alchemy is flexibility. While intentionality is essential, we must also recognize that life is unpredictable and that our plans will inevitably be disrupted. Rather than clinging rigidly to our schedules, we must embrace flexibility, adapting to unexpected challenges and opportunities as they arise. This requires us to cultivate a mindset of openness and adaptability, allowing us to navigate the inevitable twists and turns of life with grace and resilience.

Flexibility also involves recognizing that our energy levels and focus fluctuate throughout the day. By understanding our natural rhythms and adapting our activities accordingly, we can optimize our productivity and avoid burnout. For example, we may choose to tackle demanding tasks during our peak energy hours and reserve less mentally taxing activities for times when our focus is waning.

The fourth principle of Time Alchemy is mindfulness. In our fast-paced, hyper-connected world, it is easy to become disconnected from the present moment, our attention constantly pulled in a thousand different directions. Mindfulness is the practice of bringing our attention back to the present moment, fully engaging with the task at hand, and savoring the richness of our experiences.

By cultivating mindfulness, we can transform even mundane tasks into opportunities for growth and self-discovery. We can also develop a deeper appreciation for the passage of time, recognizing that each moment is a precious gift to be cherished.

Time Alchemy is not a quick fix or a magic formula. It is an ongoing process of self-discovery, experimentation, and refinement. As we deepen our understanding of ourselves and our relationship with time, we will inevitably encounter challenges and setbacks.

However, by embracing the principles of awareness, intentionality, flexibility, and mindfulness, we can transform our relationship with time into a source of empowerment and fulfillment.

In the realm of Time Alchemy, we are not passive victims of time, but active creators of our own temporal reality. We have the power to shape our days, to choose how we spend our hours and minutes, and to create a life that is rich in meaning, purpose, and joy. By embracing the principles of Time Alchemy, we can unlock the true potential of our time and transform our lives in profound ways.

ᗐᗐᗐ

The illusion of time scarcity is a self-imposed limitation. By cultivating mindfulness and focusing on the present moment, you can transcend this illusion and tap into the abundance of time that lies within.

THREE

The Time Audit: Unveiling Your Temporal Fingerprint

Time, that enigmatic entity, weaves its way through our lives, shaping our experiences, defining our routines, and leaving behind a unique imprint on each of us. This imprint, much like a fingerprint, is a testament to our individual relationship with time, reflecting our habits, priorities, and patterns of behavior. The Time Audit, a process of meticulous self-examination, offers us a profound opportunity to unveil this temporal fingerprint, to gain a deeper understanding of how we utilize this precious resource, and to identify areas where we can optimize our time management for greater productivity, fulfillment, and well-being.

The Time Audit is not merely a quantitative exercise of tracking our hours and minutes. It is a qualitative exploration of our values, goals, and aspirations. It is a journey of self-discovery, where we delve into the depths of our temporal consciousness, uncovering the hidden patterns that shape our relationship with time. By embarking on this journey, we can gain valuable insights into our strengths, weaknesses, and areas for growth, empowering us to make conscious choices about how we allocate our time and energy.

The first step in conducting a Time Audit is to create a comprehensive log of our daily activities. This can be done through various methods, such as using a time-tracking app, maintaining a detailed journal, or simply jotting down our activities at regular intervals throughout the day. The goal is to capture a snapshot of our time usage, highlighting how we allocate our hours and minutes across various domains of our lives, such as work, personal projects, relationships, leisure, and self-care.

As we meticulously record our activities, we begin to notice patterns emerging. We may discover that we spend a significant portion of our day on tasks that are not aligned with our goals or values, or that we are constantly interrupted by distractions and interruptions. We may also realize that we are neglecting certain areas of our lives, such as our health, our relationships, or our personal growth. These insights, often hidden beneath the surface of our daily routines, can be both illuminating and unsettling.

Once we have a comprehensive log of our time usage, we can begin to analyze the data, identifying areas where we can optimize our time management. This analysis can take many forms, depending on our individual needs and preferences. We may choose to categorize our activities into different buckets, such as productive, unproductive, essential, and non-essential. We may also calculate the percentage of time we spend on each activity, allowing us to visualize our time allocation in a more tangible way.

As we analyze our time usage, we may discover that we are spending a significant portion of our day on activities that are not aligned with our goals or values. For example, we may find that we are spending hours scrolling through social media, watching mindless videos, or engaging in other forms of unproductive entertainment. While these activities may provide temporary pleasure or distraction, they ultimately detract from our overall well-being and fulfillment.

To address these time leaks, we can implement various strategies, such as setting limits on our screen time, scheduling specific blocks of time for leisure activities, or replacing unproductive habits with more meaningful ones. The key is to be intentional about how we spend our time, choosing activities that align with our values and goals.

Another common finding in Time Audits is the prevalence of interruptions and distractions. In today's hyper-connected world, we are constantly bombarded with notifications, emails, and other demands on our attention. These interruptions can fragment our focus, disrupt our flow, and significantly reduce our productivity.

To mitigate the impact of interruptions, we can implement various strategies, such as setting boundaries around our work hours, turning off notifications, or creating a dedicated workspace free from distractions. We can also practice mindfulness techniques, such as meditation or deep breathing exercises, to cultivate a greater sense of focus and presence.

In addition to identifying time leaks and distractions, the Time Audit can also reveal areas of our lives that we may be neglecting. For example, we may discover that we are not spending enough time on our health, our relationships, or our personal growth. These neglected areas can lead to feelings of dissatisfaction, burnout, and even physical or mental health problems.

To address these imbalances, we can allocate specific blocks of time for activities that nourish our well-being, such as exercise, meditation, spending time with loved ones, or pursuing hobbies and passions. By prioritizing these activities, we can create a more balanced and fulfilling life.

The Time Audit is not a one-time event, but rather an ongoing process of self-reflection and adjustment. As our lives evolve, so too will our relationship with time. By regularly revisiting our Time Audit, we can ensure that our time usage remains aligned with our values, goals, and aspirations.

The benefits of conducting a Time Audit are manifold. By gaining a deeper understanding of our temporal fingerprint, we can make more conscious choices about how we allocate our time and energy. We can identify and eliminate time wasters, prioritize activities that are most meaningful to us, and create a more balanced and fulfilling life.

The Time Audit is also a powerful tool for personal growth and development. By examining our time usage patterns, we can gain valuable insights into our habits, priorities, and values. We can identify areas where we can improve our time management skills, such as delegation, prioritization, and focus. We can also develop a greater sense of self-awareness, understanding the factors that influence our decisions and behaviors.

In conclusion, the Time Audit is a transformative process that empowers us to take control of our time and create a life that is aligned with our values, goals, and aspirations. By unveiling our temporal fingerprint, we can gain valuable insights into our relationship with time, identify areas for improvement, and make conscious choices that lead to greater productivity, fulfillment, and well-being.

ᐅᐅᐅ

Goal setting is the compass that guides your journey through time. By setting clear and compelling goals, you create a roadmap for your life, ensuring that your actions are aligned with your desired outcomes.

FOUR

GOAL SETTING: YOUR COMPASS FOR TIME NAVIGATION

In the vast expanse of time, where moments stretch into hours, days into months, and years into a lifetime, it's easy to feel adrift, lost in the currents of daily life. Without a clear direction, our precious time can slip through our fingers like grains of sand, leaving us with a lingering sense of unfulfillment and regret. Goal setting, the art of defining our desired outcomes and charting a course towards them, serves as our compass for navigating the seas of time. It empowers us to take control of our temporal journey, ensuring that our efforts are aligned with our deepest aspirations and values.

At its core, goal setting is a process of self-discovery and self-creation. It involves delving into the depths of our hearts and minds, uncovering our passions, identifying our strengths, and articulating our vision for the future. By setting clear and compelling goals, we create a roadmap for our lives, a guiding light that illuminates our path and propels us forward.

The process of goal setting begins with introspection, a deep dive into our inner landscape. We ask ourselves fundamental questions: What do we truly value? What are our passions? What are our unique talents and abilities? What kind of impact do we want to make on the world? By reflecting on these questions, we begin to uncover our true north, the direction that resonates most deeply with our souls.

Once we have a clearer understanding of our values and aspirations, we can begin to articulate our goals. These goals can be specific and measurable, such as completing a marathon, writing a book, or starting a business. They can also be more general and aspirational, such as living a healthy lifestyle, building strong relationships, or making a positive contribution to society.

Regardless of their nature, effective goals share several key characteristics. They are specific, measurable, achievable, relevant, and time-bound, often referred to as SMART goals. Specific goals clearly define what we want to achieve, measurable goals allow us to track our progress, achievable goals are realistic and attainable, relevant goals align with our values and priorities, and time-bound goals create a sense of urgency and accountability.

By crafting SMART goals, we create a framework for action, a set of guidelines that help us translate our dreams into reality. We break down our goals into smaller, more manageable steps, creating a roadmap that outlines the specific actions we need to take to reach our desired outcomes. This roadmap not only provides us with a clear direction but also serves as a source of motivation, reminding us of the progress we have made and the rewards that await us at the end of our journey.

However, goal setting is not merely a matter of creating a roadmap and following it blindly. It is an iterative process that requires ongoing reflection, adjustment, and course correction. As we progress towards our goals, we inevitably encounter obstacles, setbacks, and unexpected detours. These challenges can be disheartening, but they also offer opportunities for growth and learning. By embracing a growth mindset, we can view setbacks as stepping stones to success, learning from our mistakes and adapting our strategies as needed.

Moreover, goal setting is not a solitary endeavor. It is a collaborative process that involves seeking support, guidance, and feedback from others. By sharing our goals with trusted friends, mentors, or coaches, we can gain valuable insights, encouragement, and accountability. We can also leverage the collective wisdom and experience of our community to overcome challenges and achieve our desired outcomes.

The benefits of goal setting are far-reaching and profound. Research has shown that individuals who set goals are more likely to achieve them than those who do not. Goal setting not only enhances our productivity and focus but also improves our self-confidence, resilience, and overall well-being. It empowers us to take control of our lives, to make conscious choices that align with our values and aspirations, and to create a future that is both meaningful and fulfilling.

Goal setting is not just a tool for achieving external success; it is a catalyst for personal transformation. As we strive towards our goals, we develop new skills, cultivate new habits, and expand our comfort zones. We challenge ourselves to become the best version of ourselves, to realize our full potential. In this sense, goal setting is not just about achieving a desired outcome; it is about the journey of self-discovery and self-creation that unfolds along the way.

In the tapestry of time, our goals are the threads that weave together the fabric of our lives. They give meaning and purpose to our existence, guiding us towards a future that is both fulfilling and impactful. By embracing the art of goal setting, we become the architects of our own destiny, shaping our time and creating a legacy that will endure long after we are gone.

❧❧❧

Prioritization is the art of choosing your battles wisely. By focusing your time and energy on the tasks that truly matter, you can maximize your impact and achieve your goals with greater efficiency.

FIVE

PRIORITIZATION: THE ART OF CHOOSING YOUR BATTLES WISELY

In the relentless march of time, we are constantly bombarded with an overwhelming array of tasks, responsibilities, and opportunities. The modern world, with its relentless pace and endless distractions, can easily lead us astray, leaving us feeling scattered, overwhelmed, and ultimately unfulfilled. The art of prioritization, the ability to discern the essential from the trivial, is a critical skill for navigating this chaotic landscape. It empowers us to focus our time and energy on the tasks that truly matter, ensuring that our efforts align with our values, goals, and aspirations.

Prioritization is not merely a matter of time management; it is a philosophy of life. It is about making conscious choices, aligning our actions with our intentions, and living a life that is both meaningful and purposeful. By mastering the art of prioritization, we can break free from the tyranny of urgency, overcome the allure of instant gratification, and create space for the activities that truly nourish our souls and propel us towards our goals.

At its core, prioritization is about making trade-offs. We cannot do everything at once, nor can we afford to squander our precious time and energy on pursuits that do not serve us. We must learn to discern the vital few from the trivial many, focusing our efforts on the tasks that will have the greatest impact on our lives.

The first step in mastering prioritization is to clarify our values and goals. What is truly important to us? What do we want to achieve in our lives? By defining our values and goals, we create a compass that guides our decisions and actions. When faced with a multitude of options, we can ask ourselves: "Does this task align with my values? Does it contribute to my goals?" If the answer is no, we can confidently let it go, freeing up our time and energy for more meaningful pursuits.

Once we have clarified our values and goals, we can begin to prioritize our tasks. There are numerous prioritization frameworks and techniques available, each with its own strengths and weaknesses. Some popular methods include the Eisenhower Matrix, which categorizes tasks based on their urgency and importance, and the ABCDE method, which ranks tasks based on their perceived value.

Regardless of the specific method we choose, the key is to identify the tasks that are most important and impactful. These are the tasks that will move us closer to our goals, create the most value, and have the greatest positive impact on our lives. By focusing on these high-priority tasks, we can ensure that our efforts are not wasted on trivial pursuits.

However, prioritization is not a static process. Our priorities can shift and evolve over time, depending on our circumstances and goals. We must be flexible and adaptable, adjusting our priorities as needed to ensure that we are always focusing on the tasks that are most relevant and impactful in the present moment.

One of the biggest challenges in prioritization is overcoming the tyranny of the urgent. Urgent tasks, those that demand our immediate attention, can easily hijack our days, leaving us with little time or energy for the important tasks that truly matter. We may find ourselves responding to emails, attending meetings, or dealing with crises, all while neglecting the projects that will have a lasting impact on our lives.

To overcome the tyranny of the urgent, we must learn to distinguish between urgency and importance. Urgent tasks may feel important, but they are often not. Important tasks, on the other hand, may not be urgent, but they are essential for our long-term success and well-being. By prioritizing important tasks over urgent ones, we can ensure that our efforts are focused on the things that truly matter.

Another challenge in prioritization is overcoming the allure of instant gratification. In today's world, we are constantly bombarded with temptations that promise immediate pleasure or reward. These temptations can easily derail our priorities, leading us to prioritize short-term gains over long-term goals.

To resist the allure of instant gratification, we must cultivate patience, discipline, and a long-term perspective. We must remind ourselves of our goals and values, focusing on the bigger picture rather than succumbing to the temptations of the moment. We must also develop strategies for managing our impulses and distractions, such as creating a distraction-free work environment or setting limits on our screen time.

Prioritization is not just about managing tasks; it is also about managing our energy. We all have limited energy and focus throughout the day, and it is important to allocate our energy wisely. By identifying our peak performance times and scheduling our most important tasks during those times, we can maximize our productivity and avoid burnout.

Prioritization is an ongoing process that requires constant vigilance and self-reflection. It is not always easy, but it is essential for living a life that is both meaningful and fulfilling. By mastering the art of prioritization, we can take control of our time, focus our energy on the things that truly matter, and create a life that is aligned with our values, goals, and aspirations.

ᐅᐅᐅ

Time blocking is the architect's blueprint for your day. By designing a schedule that aligns with your priorities and energy levels, you can create a framework for productivity and fulfillment.

SIX

THE EISENHOWER MATRIX: SORTING THE URGENT FROM THE IMPORTANT

In the relentless currents of time, we are constantly bombarded with an overwhelming deluge of tasks, responsibilities, and demands. The modern world, with its relentless pace and endless distractions, can easily lead us astray, leaving us feeling frazzled, overwhelmed, and ultimately unfulfilled. In the face of this ceaseless torrent of stimuli, how do we discern the truly important from the merely urgent? How do we ensure that our precious time and energy are directed towards the activities that truly matter, those that align with our values, goals, and aspirations? The Eisenhower Matrix, a simple yet powerful tool for decision-making and prioritization, offers a solution to this pervasive challenge, empowering us tonavigate the complexities of modern life with greater clarity, focus, and effectiveness.

The Eisenhower Matrix, named after former U.S. President Dwight D. Eisenhower, is a two-by-two grid that categorizes tasks based on their urgency and importance. Urgent tasks are those that demand immediate attention, while important tasks are those that contribute to our long-term goals and values. The matrix is divided into four quadrants:

Quadrant I: Urgent and Important: These are tasks that require immediate action and have significant consequences if not addressed promptly. Examples include crises, deadlines, and pressing problems.

Quadrant II: Important but Not Urgent: These are tasks that contribute to our long-term goals and values but do not have immediate deadlines. Examples include planning, relationship building, and personal development.

Quadrant III: Urgent but Not Important: These are tasks that demand immediate attention but do not contribute to our long-term goals and values. Examples include interruptions, some meetings, and certain emails.

Quadrant IV: Not Urgent and Not Important: These are tasks that neither demand immediate attention nor contribute to our long-term goals and values. Examples include busywork, time wasters, and trivial activities.

The Eisenhower Matrix provides a simple yet effective framework for prioritizing our tasks and activities. By categorizing our tasks into these four quadrants, we can quickly assess their relative importance and urgency, allowing us to make informed decisions about how to allocate our time and energy.

The most effective use of the Eisenhower Matrix is to focus our efforts on Quadrant II activities. These are the tasks that are essential for our long-term success and well-being, but are often neglected in the face of more pressing demands. By proactively scheduling time for Quadrant II activities, such as planning, learning, and relationship building, we can ensure that we are making progress towards our goals, even when faced with the inevitable distractions and interruptions of daily life.

Quadrant I activities, while important, should be managed carefully. While it is essential to address urgent and important tasks promptly, we should also strive to minimize their occurrence. This can be achieved through proactive planning, effective delegation, and the establishment of clear boundaries and expectations. By reducing the number of crises and emergencies we face, we can free up more time and energy for Quadrant II activities.

Quadrant III activities, while often demanding our immediate attention, are ultimately distractions from our most important work. It is essential to learn to identify and minimize these distractions, delegating them whenever possible or simply saying no. By reducing the amount of time we spend on Quadrant III activities, we can create more space for the tasks that truly matter.

Quadrant IV activities should be avoided altogether. These are the time wasters that drain our energy and productivity without contributing to our goals or values. By eliminating these activities from our lives, we can reclaim valuable time and resources that can be redirected towards more meaningful pursuits.

The Eisenhower Matrix is a versatile tool that can be applied to various aspects of our lives. In the workplace, it can help us prioritize projects, manage deadlines, and delegate tasks effectively. In our personal lives, it can help us focus on our health, relationships, and personal growth. By integrating the Eisenhower Matrix into our daily routines, we can transform the way we approach time management, achieving greater productivity, fulfillment, and well-being.

However, the Eisenhower Matrix is not without its limitations. It is important to recognize that the categorization of tasks into the four quadrants is subjective and can vary depending on individual values, goals, and circumstances. What is important to one person may not be important to another. Therefore, it is essential to tailor the matrix to our own specific needs and priorities.

Furthermore, the Eisenhower Matrix is not a one-size-fits-all solution to time management. It is a tool that should be used in conjunction with other strategies, such as time blocking, batching tasks, and utilizing productivity apps. By combining different approaches, we can create a comprehensive time management system that works for us.

The Eisenhower Matrix is also not a static tool. Our priorities and goals can shift and evolve over time, and it is important to regularly reassess our tasks and activities to ensure that they remain aligned with our current needs and aspirations. By periodically revisiting the matrix, we can ensure that we are always focusing on the tasks that are most important and impactful in the present moment.

Despite its limitations, the Eisenhower Matrix remains a valuable tool for anyone seeking to master the art of time management. By providing a simple yet effective framework for prioritizing our tasks and activities, it empowers us to make conscious choices about how we allocate our time and energy. By focusing on important but not urgent tasks, minimizing distractions, and eliminating time wasters, we can create a life that is both productive and fulfilling.

The Eisenhower Matrix is not just a tool for managing tasks; it is a philosophy of life. It is about making conscious choices, aligning our actions with our intentions, and living a life that is both meaningful and purposeful. By embracing this philosophy, we can break free from the tyranny of urgency, overcome the allure of instant gratification, and create space for the activities that truly nourish our souls and propel us towards our goals.

ᗐᗐᗐ

The Pomodoro Technique is a powerful tool for boosting focus and overcoming procrastination. By breaking down work into intervals separated by short breaks, you can enhance your concentration and achieve deep work.

SEVEN

TIME BLOCKING: CRAFTING YOUR PERSONALIZED TIME BLUEPRINT

In the intricate dance of life, where moments morph into hours and days into years, time remains an elusive yet precious resource. We strive to harness its power, to bend it to our will, and to maximize its potential for productivity and fulfillment. Yet, in the face of countless demands and distractions, time often slips through our fingers, leaving us feeling overwhelmed and unaccomplished. Time blocking, a strategic approach to time management, offers a solution to this pervasive challenge, empowering us to reclaim control of our schedules and create a personalized time blueprint that aligns with our values, goals, and aspirations.

Time blocking, at its core, is a simple yet powerful concept. It involves dividing our day into distinct blocks of time, each dedicated to a specific task or activity. By assigning specific time slots for various aspects of our lives, we create a structured framework that guides our actions, minimizes distractions, and maximizes our productivity.

The beauty of time blocking lies in its adaptability and personalization. Unlike rigid schedules that dictate every minute of our day, time blocking allows us to tailor our time allocation to our individual needs, preferences, and energy levels. We can create a time blueprint that reflects our unique rhythm and flow, ensuring that we are working on the right tasks at the right times.

The first step in crafting our personalized time blueprint is to identify our priorities. What are the most important tasks and activities that we need to accomplish each day? What are our long-term goals and aspirations? By clarifying our priorities, we can allocate our time accordingly, ensuring that our efforts are aligned with our values and objectives.

Once we have identified our priorities, we can begin to allocate specific time blocks for each task or activity. This involves estimating the amount of time required for each task and scheduling it into our calendar. It is important to be realistic in our time estimates, taking into account potential interruptions and distractions. We should also leave some buffer time between tasks to allow for flexibility and unexpected events.

When creating our time blocks, it is crucial to consider our natural energy levels and rhythms. We all have peak performance times when we are most alert, focused, and productive. By scheduling our most demanding tasks during these peak times, we can maximize our efficiency and minimize procrastination. Conversely, we can schedule less demanding tasks, such as emails or routine chores, during times when our energy levels are lower.

Another key aspect of time blocking is creating a dedicated workspace that is free from distractions. This may involve turning off notifications on our phones, closing unnecessary tabs on our computers, or simply finding a quiet corner where we can focus without interruption. By minimizing distractions, we can create an environment that is conducive to deep work and sustained focus.

To ensure the effectiveness of our time blocking system, it is important to review and adjust our time blueprint regularly. Our priorities and energy levels may fluctuate over time, and it is important to adapt our schedule accordingly. We can also experiment with different time blocking techniques to find what works best for us. For example, some people prefer to schedule their entire day in advance, while others prefer to block out time for specific tasks as they arise.

Time blocking offers a myriad of benefits for both our personal and professional lives. By creating a structured framework for our time, we can reduce stress and anxiety, increase productivity, and achieve our goals more efficiently. Time blocking also allows us to create more space for the things that truly matter, such as spending time with loved ones, pursuing hobbies, or simply relaxing and recharging.

One of the most significant benefits of time blocking is that it helps us overcome procrastination. By assigning specific time slots for each task, we eliminate the temptation to put things off until later. We also create a sense of urgency and accountability, motivating us to start and complete our tasks within the allotted time frame.

Time blocking also enhances our focus and concentration. By dedicating specific blocks of time to a single task, we eliminate the distractions and interruptions that can derail our productivity. We can enter a state of flow, where we are fully immersed in our work and able to achieve optimal performance.

In addition to boosting productivity, time blocking can also improve our overall well-being. By creating a structured schedule, we can reduce stress and anxiety, knowing that we have allocated time for all of our important tasks and activities. We can also create more space for rest and relaxation, which are essential for maintaining our physical and mental health.

Time blocking is a versatile tool that can be applied to various aspects of our lives. In the workplace, it can help us manage projects, meet deadlines, and collaborate effectively with colleagues. In our personal lives, it can help us prioritize our health, relationships, and personal growth. By integrating time blocking into our daily routines, we can transform the way we approach time management, achieving greater balance, fulfillment, and success.

However, it is important to note that time blocking is not a magic bullet. It requires discipline, commitment, and a willingness to experiment and adapt. We may not always be able to stick to our schedule perfectly, and that is okay. The key is to be flexible and forgiving, adjusting our time blocks as needed to accommodate unexpected events or changes in priorities.

The art of time blocking is a lifelong journey of self-discovery and refinement. As we evolve and grow, so too will our time blueprint. By embracing the principles of time blocking, we can unlock the true potential of our time, creating a life that is both productive and fulfilling.

ᗰᗰᗰ

Procrastination is the thief of time. By understanding its roots and implementing effective strategies, you can break free from its grasp and reclaim your productivity.

EIGHT

POMODORO POWER: BOOSTING FOCUS AND PRODUCTIVITY

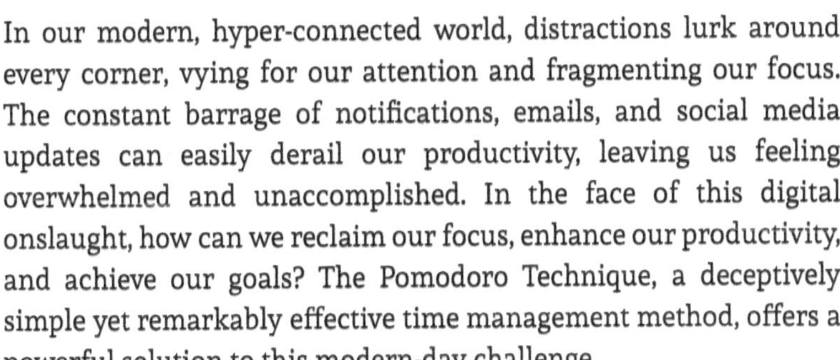

In our modern, hyper-connected world, distractions lurk around every corner, vying for our attention and fragmenting our focus. The constant barrage of notifications, emails, and social media updates can easily derail our productivity, leaving us feeling overwhelmed and unaccomplished. In the face of this digital onslaught, how can we reclaim our focus, enhance our productivity, and achieve our goals? The Pomodoro Technique, a deceptively simple yet remarkably effective time management method, offers a powerful solution to this modern-day challenge.

The Pomodoro Technique, developed by Francesco Cirillo in the late 1980s, is a time management method that breaks down work into intervals, traditionally 25 minutes in length, separated by short breaks. These intervals are named pomodoros, the Italian word for tomato, after the tomato-shaped kitchen timer Cirillo used as a university student. The technique is based on the idea that frequent breaks can improve mental agility and enhance focus, ultimately leading to increased productivity.

At its core, the Pomodoro Technique is a simple four-step process:

Choose a task: Select a task that you want to focus on. It could be anything from writing a report to answering emails to completing a creative project.

Set a timer: Set a timer for 25 minutes and work on the task without interruption until the timer rings. During this time, you should focus solely on the task at hand, avoiding all distractions.

Take a short break: When the timer rings, take a short break of 5 minutes. Get up, stretch, grab a drink, or do something else to refresh your mind and body.

Repeat: After the short break, repeat steps 1-3. After completing four pomodoros, take a longer break of 20-30 minutes.

The Pomodoro Technique's simplicity is one of its greatest strengths. It is easy to understand, implement, and adapt to individual needs and preferences. The technique can be used for any type of task, from mundane chores to complex projects. It can also be customized by adjusting the length of the work intervals and breaks to suit your personal preferences and work style.

The effectiveness of the Pomodoro Technique lies in its ability to address several key challenges to productivity. First, it helps to overcome procrastination by breaking down large, daunting tasks into smaller, more manageable chunks. This can make the task feel less overwhelming and more achievable, increasing the likelihood that we will actually start and complete it.

Second, the technique promotes deep work and sustained focus by encouraging us to eliminate distractions and concentrate solely on the task at hand. The short breaks provide an opportunity to rest and recharge, preventing mental fatigue and burnout. The regular intervals also create a sense of urgency and momentum, motivating us to work efficiently and effectively.

Third, the Pomodoro Technique can help us to improve our time management skills by providing a structured framework for our work. By tracking our pomodoros, we can gain valuable insights into our productivity patterns, identifying areas where we can improve our focus and efficiency. This data can then be used to optimize our work schedule, ensuring that we are working on the right tasks at the right times.

The Pomodoro Technique has been widely adopted by individuals and organizations across various industries, with countless success stories attesting to its effectiveness. Students use it to improve their study habits, entrepreneurs use it to manage their businesses, and creative professionals use it to overcome creative blocks and enhance their output.

While the Pomodoro Technique is a powerful tool for boosting focus and productivity, it is important to note that it is not a magic bullet. It requires discipline, commitment, and a willingness to experiment and adapt. Not every task or individual will be perfectly suited to the traditional 25-minute work intervals and 5-minute breaks. Some tasks may require longer or shorter intervals, while some individuals may prefer to work in longer stretches with longer breaks.

To maximize the benefits of the Pomodoro Technique, it is essential to customize it to your individual needs and preferences. Experiment with different interval lengths and break durations to find what works best for you. You can also try using different tools, such as a traditional kitchen timer, a smartphone app, or a browser extension, to track your pomodoros.

It is also important to be mindful of your environment and eliminate distractions as much as possible. This may involve turning off notifications on your phone, closing unnecessary tabs on your computer, or finding a quiet workspace where you can focus without interruption.

In addition to the traditional Pomodoro Technique, there are several variations and adaptations that can be explored. For example, the Pomodoro Technique can be combined with other time management methods, such as time blocking or the Eisenhower Matrix, to create a more comprehensive and personalized system.

Furthermore, the principles of the Pomodoro Technique can be applied to other areas of life beyond work. For example, it can be used to improve study habits, manage household chores, or even pursue creative hobbies. By breaking down activities into smaller, more manageable chunks and taking regular breaks, we can increase our focus, motivation, and overall effectiveness.

The Pomodoro Technique is more than just a time management method. It is a philosophy of work that emphasizes focus, intentionality, and balance. By embracing this philosophy, we can reclaim control of our time, overcome distractions, and achieve our goals with greater ease and efficiency. The Pomodoro Technique empowers us to work smarter, not harder, and to create a more productive and fulfilling life.

In a world that is constantly vying for our attention, the Pomodoro Technique offers a sanctuary of focus and productivity. It is a simple yet powerful tool that can help us to achieve our goals, enhance our well-being, and ultimately, live a more meaningful and fulfilling life.

ppp

Batching tasks is the art of efficiency through grouping. By consolidating similar activities, you can streamline your workflow, reduce distractions, and maximize your output.

NINE

OVERCOMING PROCRASTINATION: THE THIEF OF TIME

Procrastination, the insidious thief of time, lurks in the shadows of our lives, silently stealing away our precious moments and leaving behind a trail of unfulfilled promises, missed deadlines, and nagging guilt. It is a universal human experience, a struggle that transcends age, culture, and profession. From students grappling with looming assignments to entrepreneurs wrestling with business plans, procrastination casts its shadow over our endeavors, robbing us of our potential and leaving us feeling frustrated and unaccomplished. Yet, beneath its formidable facade, procrastination is not an insurmountable foe. By understanding its roots, recognizing its triggers, and implementing effective strategies, we can break free from its grasp and reclaim our time, our productivity, and our peace of mind.

At its core, procrastination is not merely laziness or a lack of willpower. It is a complex psychological phenomenon with multifaceted origins. One of the primary drivers of procrastination is the fear of failure. When faced with a challenging or daunting task, we may subconsciously delay starting it, fearing that we will not be able to meet our own expectations or the expectations of others. This fear can lead to a vicious cycle of avoidance, where we procrastinate to avoid the potential pain of failure, only to experience even greater pain and anxiety as deadlines loom and consequences mount.

Another common trigger of procrastination is a lack of clarity or direction. When we are unsure of what we need to do or how to do it, we may feel overwhelmed and paralyzed by indecision. This lack of clarity can lead to a state of inertia, where we avoid taking action because we simply do not know where to start.

In addition to fear and uncertainty, procrastination can also be fueled by a lack of motivation or interest. When we are not engaged or invested in a task, we are more likely to put it off in favor of more appealing activities. This is especially true in today's world, where countless distractions are readily available at our fingertips, from social media to streaming services to online games.

To overcome procrastination, we must first understand its underlying causes. By identifying our specific triggers and patterns of behavior, we can develop targeted strategies for breaking free from its grasp. This may involve addressing our fears and anxieties, seeking clarity and direction, or finding ways to make our tasks more engaging and meaningful.

One effective strategy for overcoming procrastination is to break down large, overwhelming tasks into smaller, more manageable steps. This can make the task feel less daunting and more achievable, increasing our motivation and reducing our anxiety. By focusing on completing one small step at a time, we can build momentum and gradually overcome our resistance to starting.

Another helpful strategy is to create a structured schedule and stick to it. By setting aside specific times for working on our tasks, we create a sense of accountability and reduce the temptation to procrastinate. We can also use time management techniques, such as the Pomodoro Technique, to break our work into intervals with short breaks, promoting focus and preventing burnout.

In addition to these practical strategies, it is also important to address the underlying emotional and psychological factors that contribute to procrastination. This may involve challenging our negative self-talk, developing a more positive and empowering mindset, and seeking support from friends, family, or professionals.

One of the most powerful tools for overcoming procrastination is self-compassion. We all procrastinate from time to time, and it is important to be kind to ourselves when we do. Instead of berating ourselves for our shortcomings, we can acknowledge our struggles, learn from our mistakes, and move forward with renewed determination.

Furthermore, it is important to cultivate a sense of self-efficacy, the belief that we have the ability to accomplish our goals. This can be achieved by setting realistic goals, breaking down tasks into manageable steps, and celebrating our successes along the way. By building our confidence and self-belief, we can overcome our fears and doubts, and take bold action towards our goals.

Overcoming procrastination is not a one-time event; it is an ongoing process of self-awareness, self-regulation, and self-compassion. It requires us to be mindful of our thoughts, feelings, and behaviors, and to make conscious choices that align with our values and goals. By cultivating these skills, we can transform procrastination from a debilitating obstacle into a catalyst for growth and transformation.

In the grand tapestry of time, procrastination is a thread that can either unravel our potential or weave a pattern of resilience and triumph. By understanding its roots, recognizing its triggers, and implementing effective strategies, we can break free from its grasp and reclaim our time, our productivity, and our peace of mind. We can transform procrastination from a thief of time into a teacher of valuable life lessons, empowering us to live a life that is both meaningful and fulfilling.

ppp

Delegation is the multiplier of time. By entrusting tasks to others, you can free up your own time and energy for more strategic and high-impact activities.

TEN

BATCHING TASKS: EFFICIENCY THROUGH GROUPING

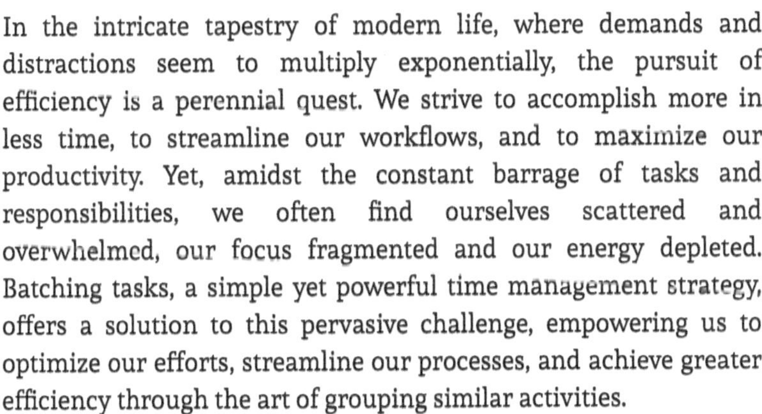

In the intricate tapestry of modern life, where demands and distractions seem to multiply exponentially, the pursuit of efficiency is a perennial quest. We strive to accomplish more in less time, to streamline our workflows, and to maximize our productivity. Yet, amidst the constant barrage of tasks and responsibilities, we often find ourselves scattered and overwhelmed, our focus fragmented and our energy depleted. Batching tasks, a simple yet powerful time management strategy, offers a solution to this pervasive challenge, empowering us to optimize our efforts, streamline our processes, and achieve greater efficiency through the art of grouping similar activities.

Batching tasks, also known as task grouping or clustering, is the practice of completing similar tasks together in one concentrated effort, rather than switching back and forth between different types of activities. This approach leverages the power of context switching, the mental process of transitioning from one task to another. By minimizing context switching, we reduce the cognitive load associated with task transitions, allowing us to focus more deeply on each task and complete it more efficiently.

The concept of batching tasks is not a new one. It has been employed in various industries for centuries, from manufacturing assembly lines to restaurant kitchens. The underlying principle is simple: by grouping similar tasks together, we can eliminate unnecessary setup and transition time, streamline our workflow, and ultimately increase our output.

In the realm of personal productivity, batching tasks can be applied to a wide range of activities. For example, we can batch our emails by setting aside specific times of day to check and respond to messages, rather than constantly interrupting our work to attend to incoming emails. We can batch our errands by grouping together tasks that require us to be in the same location, such as grocery shopping, picking up dry cleaning, and running other errands in the same neighborhood. We can even batch our creative work by dedicating specific blocks of time to brainstorming, writing, or designing, allowing us to enter a state of flow and maximize our creative output.

The benefits of batching tasks are manifold. First and foremost, it can significantly increase our productivity. By minimizing context switching, we reduce the mental friction associated with task transitions, allowing us to focus more deeply on each task and complete it more quickly and efficiently. This can lead to a significant reduction in the time required to complete a set of tasks, freeing up valuable time for other activities.

Second, batching tasks can help us to improve the quality of our work. When we focus on one type of task at a time, we can develop a rhythm and momentum that can lead to higher quality output. We are less likely to make mistakes or overlook important details when we are fully immersed in a particular task.

Third, batching tasks can reduce stress and overwhelm. When we are constantly switching between different types of tasks, we can feel scattered and unfocused. This can lead to stress, anxiety, and a sense of being overwhelmed by our workload. By batching tasks, we create a sense of order and control, knowing that we have dedicated time for each type of activity. This can help us to feel more calm, focused, and in control of our time.

Fourth, batching tasks can improve our time management skills. By consciously grouping similar tasks together, we become more aware of how we spend our time and how long it takes us to complete different types of activities. This awareness can help us to make more informed decisions about how to allocate our time and prioritize our tasks.

To effectively implement batching tasks, there are several key strategies we can employ. First, we must identify the tasks that are most amenable to batching. These are typically tasks that are similar in nature, require similar resources or tools, or can be completed in the same location. For example, writing emails, making phone calls, and attending meetings are all tasks that can be easily batched together.

Second, we must create a schedule that allocates specific time blocks for different types of tasks. This may involve setting aside dedicated time for email, meetings, creative work, or administrative tasks. By scheduling these time blocks in advance, we create a structure for our day that minimizes distractions and maximizes focus.

Third, we must be disciplined in adhering to our schedule. It can be tempting to deviate from our plan and switch between tasks as they arise, but this can quickly undermine the benefits of batching. By sticking to our schedule, we train our minds to focus on one type of task at a time, leading to increased efficiency and productivity.

Fourth, we must be flexible and adaptable. While it is important to have a schedule, we must also be willing to adjust it as needed. Unexpected events or urgent tasks may require us to deviate from our plan, but we should strive to return to our batching schedule as soon as possible.

Batching tasks is not a one-size-fits-all solution. The optimal approach will vary depending on individual preferences, work styles, and the nature of the tasks involved. Some people may prefer to batch tasks on a daily basis, while others may find it more effective to batch tasks on a weekly or monthly basis. The key is to experiment with different approaches and find what works best for you.

The benefits of batching tasks extend beyond increased productivity and efficiency. By creating a more structured and focused approach to our work, we can reduce stress, improve our time management skills, and create more space for the activities that truly matter to us. Whether we are students, professionals, entrepreneurs, or simply individuals seeking to maximize our time and energy, batching tasks can be a powerful tool for achieving our goals and living a more fulfilling life.

In the grand symphony of life, where countless notes and melodies compete for our attention, batching tasks is akin to arranging the music into harmonious chords. By grouping similar tasks together, we create a sense of order and coherence, allowing us to navigate the complexities of modern life with greater ease and grace. Through the art of batching tasks, we can transform the cacophony of competing demands into a symphony of productivity, efficiency, and fulfillment.

❦❦❦

The power of saying "no" is the guardian of your time. By learning to decline requests and opportunities that do not align with your values and goals, you can reclaim your autonomy and protect your precious time.

ELEVEN

DELEGATION: THE MULTIPLIER OF TIME

In the intricate dance of time, where moments are fleeting and opportunities abound, the pursuit of maximizing our impact and achieving our goals often feels like a race against the clock. We strive to do more, be more, and accomplish more, yet the limitations of our individual capacity can hinder our progress. Delegation, the art of entrusting tasks and responsibilities to others, emerges as a powerful tool for expanding our reach, multiplying our time, and achieving exponential growth. It is a skill that transcends individual effort, enabling us to leverage the collective talents and expertise of others to achieve outcomes that would be impossible alone.

At its core, delegation is not merely about offloading tasks or avoiding work. It is a strategic approach to leadership, collaboration, and empowerment. It is about recognizing the unique strengths and capabilities of each individual and assigning tasks that align with their skills and interests. By delegating effectively, we not only free up our own time and energy for higher-level activities but also foster a sense of ownership and accountability among our team members, leading to increased engagement, motivation, and overall performance.

The art of delegation begins with a shift in mindset. We must move beyond the notion that we must do everything ourselves, that we are the sole custodians of our success. Instead, we must embrace the idea that we can achieve far more by empowering others, by leveraging their talents and expertise to complement our own. This requires a willingness to let go of control, to trust in the abilities of others, and to create an environment where everyone feels valued and empowered to contribute their best.

To delegate effectively, we must first identify the tasks that are most suitable for delegation. These are typically tasks that are repetitive, time-consuming, or require specialized skills that we may not possess. By delegating these tasks, we can free up our own time and energy for more strategic, creative, or high-impact activities that align with our core competencies.

Once we have identified the tasks to delegate, we must carefully select the individuals who are best suited to take them on. This involves considering their skills, experience, interests, and availability. It is important to choose individuals who are capable of completing the task successfully and who are motivated to take on the responsibility. By matching the right task with the right person, we can ensure that the task is completed efficiently and effectively, while also providing opportunities for growth and development for our team members.

Effective delegation is not simply about assigning tasks and walking away. It requires clear communication, ongoing support, and regular feedback. When delegating a task, we must clearly articulate our expectations, providing detailed instructions, deadlines, and resources. We must also be available to answer questions, provide guidance, and offer support as needed. By fostering open communication and collaboration, we can ensure that the task is completed to our satisfaction, while also empowering our team members to take ownership of their work and develop their skills.

Regular feedback is also essential for effective delegation. By providing constructive feedback on both successes and challenges, we can help our team members learn and grow, while also ensuring that the task is on track and meeting our expectations. Feedback should be specific, timely, and focused on both outcomes and behaviors. By providing regular feedback, we can foster a culture of continuous improvement and empower our team members to reach their full potential.

Delegation is not without its challenges. One common obstacle is the fear of losing control. We may worry that if we delegate a task, it will not be done to our standards, or that we will lose visibility into the progress of the work. This fear can lead us to micromanage our team members, undermining their autonomy and hindering their growth. To overcome this fear, we must cultivate trust in the abilities of others, provide clear guidelines and expectations, and create a system for regular communication and feedback.

Another challenge is the resistance from team members. Some individuals may be hesitant to take on new responsibilities, fearing that they will not be able to succeed or that they will be overwhelmed by the additional workload. To address this resistance, we must provide adequate training and support, clearly communicate the benefits of delegation, and create a culture where taking on new challenges is encouraged and rewarded.

The benefits of delegation are numerous and far-reaching. For the individual, delegation can free up valuable time and energy for more strategic, creative, or high-impact activities. It can also lead to reduced stress, improved work-life balance, and greater job satisfaction. For the team, delegation can foster a sense of ownership, accountability, and empowerment. It can also promote skill development, collaboration, and innovation. For the organization, delegation can lead to increased productivity, improved efficiency, and enhanced competitiveness.

Delegation is not just a tool for time management; it is a catalyst for growth and transformation. By empowering others, we not only multiply our own time and impact but also create a ripple effect of positive change that can extend throughout our organizations and communities. Delegation is an investment in the future, a way of building capacity, developing talent, and creating a legacy that will endure long after we are gone.

In the grand tapestry of life, time is the most precious thread, and delegation is the loom that allows us to weave a masterpiece of accomplishment. By entrusting tasks and responsibilities to others, we unleash the power of collaboration, amplify our impact, and create a world where everyone can thrive. Delegation is not merely a strategy; it is a philosophy of leadership, a commitment to empowerment, and a testament to the boundless potential of human collaboration.

ቦቦቦ

Mindful time management is the practice of being fully present in each moment. By cultivating awareness and non-judgment, you can transform your relationship with time and create a life of greater peace and purpose.

TWELVE

THE POWER OF SAYING NO: PROTECTING YOUR PRECIOUS TIME

In the relentless currents of modern life, where demands and distractions seem to multiply exponentially, the pursuit of productivity and fulfillment can often feel like an endless uphill battle. We are constantly bombarded with requests, invitations, and obligations, each vying for our precious time and attention. The allure of saying "yes" to every opportunity, every request, and every invitation can be seductive, promising a life filled with excitement, connection, and achievement. Yet, this relentless pursuit of "yes" can lead us down a treacherous path, one paved with burnout, overwhelm, and a nagging sense of unfulfillment. It is in the art of saying "no" that we discover the true power to protect our precious time, to reclaim our autonomy, and to cultivate a life that aligns with our values, goals, and aspirations.

Saying "no" is not a sign of weakness or selfishness; it is a testament to our self-awareness, our discernment, and our unwavering commitment to our own well-being. It is a declaration of our sovereignty over our time, an assertion of our right to choose how we spend our days, and a refusal to be swept away by the tide of external demands.

The power of saying "no" lies in its ability to create space. When we say "no" to something, we are not merely rejecting a particular request or opportunity; we are creating space for something else. We are opening up our lives to new possibilities, new experiences, and new perspectives. By consciously choosing what we say "yes" to, we are also implicitly choosing what we say "no" to.

In the realm of time management, the power of saying "no" is paramount. Every "yes" we utter comes at a cost, a sacrifice of our time, energy, and attention. When we say "yes" to everything, we are essentially spreading ourselves too thin, diluting our focus, and diminishing our effectiveness. By learning to say "no" to the non-essential, we can reclaim our time and energy for the things that truly matter, those activities that align with our values, goals, and aspirations.

Saying "no" is not always easy. We may fear disappointing others, missing out on opportunities, or being perceived as uncooperative or unhelpful. We may also feel obligated to say "yes" out of a sense of duty, guilt, or social pressure. However, the long-term consequences of saying "yes" to everything can be far more detrimental than the short-term discomfort of saying "no."

To cultivate the power of saying "no," we must first develop a deep understanding of our own values, goals, and priorities. What is truly important to us? What do we want to achieve in our lives? By clarifying our values and goals, we create a compass that guides our decisions and actions. When faced with a request or opportunity, we can ask ourselves: "Does this align with my values? Does it contribute to my goals?" If the answer is no, we can confidently say "no," knowing that we are protecting our precious time and energy for the things that truly matter.

Saying "no" is not about being rude or dismissive. It is about communicating our boundaries with clarity and respect. When declining a request, we can express our appreciation for the opportunity, explain our reasons for declining, and offer alternative solutions if appropriate. By communicating our "no" with grace and diplomacy, we can maintain positive relationships while still protecting our time and energy.

The art of saying "no" is a skill that can be developed and refined over time. It requires practice, self-awareness, and a willingness to challenge our own beliefs and assumptions. We may need to overcome our fear of missing out, our desire to please others, and our tendency to overcommit. However, the rewards of mastering this skill are immense.

When we learn to say "no," we reclaim our autonomy and take control of our lives. We free ourselves from the tyranny of external demands and create space for the things that truly matter. We become more focused, more productive, and more fulfilled. We also set a positive example for others, demonstrating that it is okay to prioritize our own well-being and to say "no" when necessary.

The power of saying "no" is not just about protecting our time; it is about protecting our energy, our focus, and our sanity. When we say "yes" to everything, we deplete our resources, scatter our attention, and create unnecessary stress and overwhelm. By saying "no" to the non-essential, we conserve our energy for the things that truly matter, allowing us to show up fully for the people and activities we care about most.

In the grand symphony of life, saying "no" is not a discordant note, but a harmonious pause. It is a moment of silence that allows us to hear our own inner voice, to discern our true desires, and to make choices that align with our deepest values. By embracing the power of saying "no," we can create a life that is both rich in meaning and abundant in joy.

◁◁◁

*Digital time management tools are your allies in
the quest for productivity. By harnessing their
power, you can streamline your workflow, track
your progress, and achieve your goals with greater
ease and efficiency.*

THIRTEEN

MINDFUL TIME MANAGEMENT: HARNESSING THE PRESENT MOMENT

In our modern, fast-paced world, the relentless pursuit of productivity often leaves us feeling overwhelmed, stressed, and disconnected from the present moment. We are constantly bombarded with distractions, deadlines, and demands, leaving us with little time to simply be. In the midst of this chaotic whirlwind, mindfulness emerges as a powerful antidote, a beacon of calm and clarity that can transform our relationship with time and empower us to live more fulfilling and purposeful lives. Mindful time management, the art of integrating mindfulness practices into our daily routines, offers a revolutionary approach to navigating the complexities of modern life, enabling us to harness the power of the present moment and cultivate a deeper sense of peace, focus, and well-being.

Mindfulness, at its core, is the practice of paying attention to the present moment without judgment. It is about cultivating a nonreactive awareness of our thoughts, feelings, and sensations, allowing us to fully engage with the world around us and make conscious choices about how we spend our time and energy. By integrating mindfulness into our time management practices, we can transcend the reactive, autopilot mode that often governs our lives, and create space for intentionality, creativity, and joy.

The first step in mindful time management is to cultivate present moment awareness. This involves developing the ability to anchor our attention in the here and now, rather than dwelling on past regrets or future anxieties. Mindfulness practices, such as meditation, deep breathing exercises, and mindful movement, can help us to cultivate this awareness, allowing us to fully experience each moment as it unfolds.

When we are fully present, we are better able to identify our priorities, make conscious choices about how we spend our time, and respond to challenges with greater clarity and resilience. We are also more likely to notice the subtle cues that our bodies and minds provide, allowing us to adjust our pace and avoid burnout.

Another key aspect of mindful time management is the cultivation of non-judgmental awareness. When we are caught up in the relentless pursuit of productivity, we often judge ourselves harshly for perceived shortcomings or failures. This self-criticism can lead to stress, anxiety, and a sense of inadequacy. By cultivating a non-judgmental attitude towards ourselves and our experiences, we can break free from this cycle of negativity and create space for self-compassion and acceptance.

When we approach our tasks with a non-judgmental attitude, we are more likely to be open to new ideas, embrace challenges, and learn from our mistakes. We are also more likely to find joy and satisfaction in our work, even when faced with setbacks or obstacles.

Mindful time management also involves setting intentions for how we want to spend our time. This involves identifying our values, goals, and priorities, and aligning our actions with these deeper intentions. When we set intentions for our time, we are more likely to make choices that are in alignment with our values, leading to a greater sense of purpose and fulfillment.

Intentions can be set for specific tasks, such as completing a project or attending a meeting, or for broader aspects of our lives, such as cultivating healthy relationships or pursuing personal growth. By setting intentions, we create a roadmap for our time, guiding us towards the activities that are most meaningful and impactful.

To effectively manage our time mindfully, it is also important to develop healthy boundaries. In today's hyper-connected world, it can be challenging to disconnect from work and other demands on our time. However, setting clear boundaries between our personal and professional lives is essential for maintaining our well-being and preventing burnout.

This may involve setting specific work hours, establishing a dedicated workspace, and limiting distractions, such as checking emails or social media outside of designated times. By creating clear boundaries, we protect our time and energy, ensuring that we have adequate time for rest, relaxation, and personal pursuits.

Mindful time management also involves cultivating a sense of gratitude for the time we have. In our fast-paced world, it is easy to take time for granted, to focus on what we lack rather than what we have. By cultivating gratitude for the present moment, we can shift our perspective from one of scarcity to one of abundance.

This can be achieved through simple practices, such as taking a few moments each day to reflect on the things we are grateful for, expressing appreciation for the people in our lives, or simply savoring the small joys of daily life. By cultivating gratitude, we can deepen our appreciation for the gift of time and live more fully in the present moment.

The benefits of mindful time management are manifold. By cultivating present moment awareness, non-judgmental acceptance, clear intentions, healthy boundaries, and gratitude, we can transform our relationship with time and create a life that is more balanced, fulfilling, and purposeful. We can reduce stress, increase productivity, improve our relationships, and enhance our overall well-being.

Mindful time management is not a quick fix or a magic bullet. It is an ongoing practice that requires patience, commitment, and a willingness to embrace the present moment with all its challenges and opportunities. By integrating mindfulness into our daily routines, we can unlock the true potential of our time and create a life that is rich in meaning, purpose, and joy.

ᖬᖬᖬ

Energy management is the foundation of sustainable productivity. By prioritizing your physical, mental, and emotional well-being, you can fuel your productivity engine and achieve peak performance.

FOURTEEN

TIME MANAGEMENT TOOLS: YOUR DIGITAL ALLIES

In the digital age, where information flows at an unprecedented pace and distractions abound, the quest for effective time management has become more challenging than ever. Fortunately, the same technological advancements that often contribute to our time scarcity have also given rise to a plethora of digital tools designed to help us reclaim control of our schedules, enhance our productivity, and achieve our goals with greater ease and efficiency. These digital allies, ranging from simple calendar apps to sophisticated project management platforms, have revolutionized the way we manage our time, offering us a wide array of features and functionalities that can be tailored to our individual needs and preferences.

One of the most fundamental digital time management tools is the calendar app. Whether it's the built-in calendar on our smartphones or a dedicated app like Google Calendar or Outlook, calendars provide a visual representation of our time, allowing us to schedule appointments, set reminders, and track deadlines. The beauty of calendar apps lies in their flexibility and customizability. We can create recurring events, set color-coded categories for different types of activities, and even share our calendars with others for seamless collaboration.

Calendar apps also offer features such as time zone support, which is invaluable for those who work with colleagues or clients in different parts of the world. Additionally, many calendar apps integrate with other productivity tools, such as email and task management apps, allowing us to streamline our workflow and consolidate our information in one central location.

Another essential digital ally in our quest for effective time management is the task management app. These apps, such as Todoist, Asana, and Trello, provide a centralized platform for organizing and tracking our tasks, projects, and goals. We can create to-do lists, set due dates, assign priorities, and track our progress in real-time. Many task management apps also offer features such as collaboration tools, file sharing, and integrations with other productivity apps.

One of the key benefits of task management apps is that they help us to break down large, complex projects into smaller, more manageable tasks. This can make daunting projects feel less overwhelming and more achievable. Task management apps also allow us to visualize our progress, providing a sense of accomplishment and motivation as we complete each task.

For those who struggle with procrastination, time tracking apps can be a game-changer. These apps, such as Toggl, Harvest, and RescueTime, allow us to track how we spend our time on different tasks and activities. By analyzing our time usage data, we can identify time sinks, optimize our workflow, and develop more efficient habits.

Time tracking apps can also be used to bill clients accurately, monitor project progress, and gain valuable insights into our productivity patterns. Some time tracking apps even offer features such as idle time detection, which can help us to identify and eliminate distractions.

In addition to calendar, task management, and time tracking apps, there are countless other digital tools that can enhance our time management efforts. Note-taking apps, such as Evernote and OneNote, provide a digital repository for capturing ideas, organizing information, and creating to-do lists. Communication tools, such as Slack and Microsoft Teams, streamline communication and collaboration, reducing the need for time-consuming meetings and emails. Project management platforms, such as Basecamp and Monday.com, offer a centralized platform for managing projects, tracking progress, and collaborating with team members.

Choosing the right digital time management tools can be a daunting task. With so many options available, it is important to consider our individual needs, preferences, and budget. We should also consider the features and functionalities that are most important to us, such as ease of use, cross-platform compatibility, and integrations with other tools.

It is also important to remember that digital tools are not a substitute for good time management habits. They are simply tools that can help us to implement and reinforce those habits. To truly master time management, we must develop a disciplined approach to planning, prioritizing, and executing our tasks.

Furthermore, it is important to be mindful of the potential downsides of digital time management tools. While these tools can be incredibly helpful, they can also become a source of distraction and overwhelm if not used judiciously. It is essential to set clear boundaries around our use of technology, to avoid constantly checking notifications or getting sucked into the endless scroll of social media.

In conclusion, digital time management tools can be powerful allies in our quest for productivity and fulfillment. By providing us with a visual representation of our time, a centralized platform for organizing our tasks, and valuable insights into our productivity patterns, these tools can help us to optimize our workflow, achieve our goals, and create a more balanced and meaningful life. However, it is important to remember that these tools are not a substitute for good time management habits, and that they should be used mindfully and intentionally to truly harness their transformative power.

Rest is not the enemy of productivity, but its essential counterpart. By prioritizing rest and relaxation, you can recharge your batteries, enhance your creativity, and achieve greater long-term success.

FIFTEEN

Energy Management: Fueling Your Productivity Engine

In the intricate dance of productivity, energy is the fuel that propels us forward, the lifeblood that sustains our efforts, and the spark that ignites our creativity. While time management is often hailed as the cornerstone of personal effectiveness, energy management is the often-overlooked key to unlocking our full potential. Unlike time, which is a finite and linear resource, energy is a dynamic and renewable force that can be cultivated, nurtured, and optimized to achieve peak performance and sustained well-being.

Energy management is the art and science of harnessing, directing, and renewing our physical, mental, and emotional resources to achieve optimal performance and well-being. It is a holistic approach that recognizes the interconnectedness of our various energy systems and the importance of maintaining a healthy balance between expenditure and replenishment.

Physical energy is the foundation upon which all other forms of energy rest. It is the fuel that powers our bodies, enabling us to move, think, and create. The quality of our physical energy is influenced by a multitude of factors, including nutrition, sleep, exercise, and stress management. By prioritizing these aspects of our lives, we can cultivate a strong and resilient physical energy that supports our productivity and well-being.

Nutrition plays a crucial role in energy management. The foods we eat provide the raw materials for our bodies to generate energy. A diet rich in whole, unprocessed foods, such as fruits, vegetables, whole grains, and lean proteins, provides sustained energy throughout the day, while processed foods, sugary drinks, and excessive caffeine can lead to energy crashes and fluctuations.

Sleep is another critical component of physical energy management. When we sleep, our bodies repair and restore themselves, preparing us for the challenges of the day ahead. Chronic sleep deprivation can lead to fatigue, irritability, impaired cognitive function, and a host of other health problems. By prioritizing sleep and establishing healthy sleep habits, such as maintaining a consistent sleep schedule and creating a relaxingbedtime routine, we can ensure that we wake up feeling refreshed and energized.

Exercise is not only essential for physical health but also plays a vital role in energy management. Regular physical activity can boost energy levels, improve mood, reduce stress, and enhance cognitive function. Even moderate exercise, such as brisk walking or yoga, can have a significant impact on our energy levels and overall well-being.

Stress, both acute and chronic, can drain our physical energy reserves. When we are stressed, our bodies release cortisol, a stress hormone that can interfere with sleep, digestion, and immune function. By developing effective stress management techniques, such as meditation, deep breathing exercises, or spending time in nature, we can reduce the negative impact of stress on our energy levels.

Mental energy is the fuel that powers our minds, enabling us to think clearly, focus intently, and make sound decisions. Like physical energy, mental energy is a finite resource that can be depleted through overuse and neglect. To optimize our mental energy, we must learn to manage our cognitive load, prioritize our tasks, and create an environment that is conducive to deep work.

One effective strategy for managing cognitive load is to break down large, complex tasks into smaller, more manageable chunks. This can make the task feel less daunting and more achievable, reducing cognitive overload and increasing focus. We can also utilize tools such as to-do lists, mind maps, and project management software to organize our thoughts and prioritize our tasks.

Creating a distraction-free environment is also crucial for optimizing mental energy. This may involve turning off notifications on our devices, closing unnecessary tabs on our computers, or finding a quiet workspace where we can focus without interruption. By minimizing distractions, we can create the mental space necessary for deep work and sustained focus.

Emotional energy is the fuel that powers our relationships, our creativity, and our passion for life. When our emotional energy is high, we feel positive, motivated, and engaged. When it is low, we may feel apathetic, discouraged, or even depressed. To cultivate emotional energy, we must prioritize self-care, nurture our relationships, and engage in activities that bring us joy and fulfillment.

Self-care is an essential component of emotional energy management. This can involve activities such as exercise, meditation, spending time in nature, pursuing hobbies, or simply taking time for rest and relaxation. By prioritizing self-care, we replenish our emotional reserves and cultivate a sense of well-being that radiates into all areas of our lives.

Nurturing our relationships is another key aspect of emotional energy management. Positive social interactions can boost our mood, reduce stress, and provide us with a sense of belonging and support. Conversely, negative relationships can drain our energy and leave us feeling depleted. By prioritizing healthy relationships and investing time and energy in cultivating meaningful connections, we can enhance our emotional well-being and create a supportive network that fuels our personal and professional growth.

Engaging in activities that bring us joy and fulfillment is also essential for cultivating emotional energy. Whether it is pursuing a creative hobby, volunteering for a cause we care about, or simply spending time with loved ones, these activities can spark our passion, ignite our creativity, and infuse our lives with meaning and purpose.

Energy management is a dynamic and ongoing process that requires constant awareness, experimentation, and adaptation. As our lives evolve, so too will our energy needs and priorities. By paying attention to the signals our bodies and minds provide, we can learn to adjust our behaviors and habits to optimize our energy levels and achieve peak performance.

In the grand symphony of life, energy is the conductor's baton, guiding the rhythm and tempo of our existence. By mastering the art of energy management, we can orchestrate a harmonious melody of productivity, fulfillment, and well-being, ensuring that we have the energy to pursue our passions, achieve our goals, and make a meaningful impact on the world.

ᴆᴆᴆ

Creating rituals is the key to time management on autopilot. By establishing intentional and repetitive actions, you can automate your decision-making processes and free up your mental energy for more important tasks.

SIXTEEN

THE IMPORTANCE OF REST: RECHARGING YOUR BATTERIES

In the relentless pursuit of productivity and achievement, we often find ourselves caught in a whirlwind of activity, pushing our bodies and minds to their limits. We work long hours, juggle multiple responsibilities, and strive to squeeze every last drop of efficiency from our days. Yet, in this relentless pursuit of progress, we often overlook a fundamental truth: rest is not the antithesis of productivity, but rather its essential counterpart. Rest is not a luxury, but a necessity. It is the vital pause that allows us to recharge our batteries, replenish our energy, and return to our tasks with renewed vigor and focus.

Rest is not merely the absence of activity. It is a multi-faceted concept that encompasses physical, mental, and emotional rejuvenation. Physical rest involves giving our bodies the time and space they need to recover from exertion, repair damaged tissues, and replenish energy stores. Mental rest involves disengaging from work and other mentally demanding activities, allowing our minds to wander, daydream, and process information. Emotional rest involves creating space for our emotions to be felt and processed, allowing us to release stress, anxiety, and other negative emotions that can accumulate over time.

The importance of rest for our physical health cannot be overstated. When we exert ourselves physically, whether through exercise, manual labor, or simply the daily wear and tear of life, our bodies undergo a process of breakdown and repair. During periods of rest, our bodies repair damaged tissues, rebuild muscle fibers, and replenish energy stores. This process is essential for maintaining our physical health, preventing injuries, and ensuring that we have the energy to tackle the challenges of daily life.

Sleep is perhaps the most crucial form of physical rest. During sleep, our bodies undergo a complex series of processes that are essential for our health and well-being. Our brains consolidate memories, our immune systems strengthen, and our bodies repair damaged tissues. Chronic sleep deprivation can lead to a host of health problems, including obesity, diabetes, heart disease, and even premature death.

In addition to sleep, other forms of physical rest are also important for maintaining our health and well-being. These include taking breaks throughout the day to stretch, move around, and rest our eyes, as well as engaging in regular exercise and relaxation techniques, such as yoga, meditation, or massage.

Rest is not only essential for our physical health but also plays a vital role in our mental and emotional well-being. When we are constantly engaged in mentally demanding activities, our brains become fatigued, leading to decreased focus, impaired decision-making, and increased stress. Mental rest, in the form of breaks, relaxation, and leisure activities, allows our brains to recharge, process information, and consolidate memories.

One of the most effective forms of mental rest is simply allowing our minds to wander. When we disengage from focused tasks and allow our thoughts to flow freely, we tap into our subconscious mind, where creative insights and solutions often emerge. Daydreaming, taking a walk in nature, or engaging in a hobby can all provide valuable opportunities for mental rest and rejuvenation.

Emotional rest is often overlooked but is just as important as physical and mental rest. When we are constantly bombarded with stress, anxiety, and other negative emotions, our emotional reserves can become depleted, leading to burnout, irritability, and difficulty coping with challenges. Emotional rest involves creating space for our emotions to be felt and processed, allowing us to release pent-up emotions and cultivate a greater sense of inner peace.

This can be achieved through a variety of practices, such as journaling, talking to a trusted friend or therapist, spending time in nature, or engaging in activities that bring us joy and relaxation. By prioritizing emotional rest, we can improve our mood, reduce stress, and strengthen our resilience in the face of adversity.

The benefits of rest extend beyond our physical, mental, and emotional well-being. Rest can also enhance our productivity, creativity, and overall performance. When we are well-rested, we are more focused, alert, and creative. We are better able to solve problems, make decisions, and come up with innovative ideas. We are also more likely to be engaged and motivated in our work, leading to increased productivity and better outcomes.

Research has shown that taking breaks throughout the day can actually improve our productivity. When we work for extended periods without rest, our performance begins to decline. However, by taking short breaks to rest our minds and bodies, we can maintain our focus and energy levels throughout the day.

Furthermore, rest can enhance our creativity. When we step away from a problem or task and allow our minds to wander, we often gain new insights and perspectives. This can lead to breakthrough ideas and creative solutions that we may not have discovered if we had continued to work without rest.

In addition to improving productivity and creativity, rest can also enhance our overall well-being. When we are well-rested, we are more likely to feel happy, content, and fulfilled. We are better able to manage stress, build strong relationships, and enjoy the simple pleasures of life.

In our culture of busyness and productivity, rest is often undervalued and even stigmatized. We are taught to believe that we must be constantly working and striving to achieve our goals. However, this relentless pursuit of productivity can be counterproductive in the long run. By prioritizing rest, we are not only investing in our well-being but also in our long-term success and happiness.

Rest is not a luxury; it is a necessity. It is the vital pause that allows us to recharge our batteries, replenish our energy, and return to our tasks with renewed vigor and focus. By prioritizing rest, we can improve our physical, mental, and emotional health, enhance our productivity and creativity, and ultimately, live a more fulfilling and purposeful life.

ᗡᗡᗡ

The 80/20 Rule reveals that a small fraction of our efforts often yields the majority of our results. By focusing on the vital few tasks that truly matter, you can achieve exponential results with less effort.

SEVENTEEN

Creating Rituals: Time Management on Autopilot

In the intricate dance of life, where moments seamlessly weave into hours and days into years, the quest for mastering time management often feels like an elusive pursuit. We strive to optimize our schedules, maximize our productivity, and achieve our goals, yet the relentless demands of modern life can easily derail our best intentions. Amidst the chaos and unpredictability, the creation of rituals emerges as a powerful tool for reclaiming control of our time, streamlining our routines, and fostering a sense of order and purpose in our daily lives. Rituals, those intentional, repetitive actions that we incorporate into our daily routines, serve as anchors in the sea of time, providing structure, stability, and a sense of grounding amidst the ebb and flow of life.

Rituals are not merely mindless habits or rote routines. They are deliberate acts infused with meaning and intention. They are the conscious choices we make to prioritize our well-being, to cultivate our passions, and to create space for the activities that truly matter. By incorporating rituals into our lives, we create a framework for time management that operates on autopilot, freeing up our mental energy for more creative and fulfilling pursuits.

The power of rituals lies in their ability to automate our decision-making processes. When we establish a ritual, we are essentially creating a pre-determined course of action that we follow without having to consciously think about it. This frees up our mental bandwidth for more important tasks, reducing decision fatigue and enhancing our overall productivity.

For example, if we establish a morning ritual that involves meditation, exercise, and journaling, we no longer have to decide what to do first thing in the morning. We simply follow the established routine, allowing our minds to focus on the task at hand without being bogged down by decision-making. This not only saves us time and energy but also helps us to cultivate consistency and discipline, two essential ingredients for success in any endeavor.

Rituals also serve as powerful anchors in our daily lives. They provide a sense of structure and stability amidst the chaos and unpredictability of the modern world. When we have established rituals, we know what to expect, we have a sense of control over our time, and we are less likely to be thrown off course by unexpected events. This sense of grounding can be particularly valuable during times of stress or transition, when our routines are disrupted and our sense of control is challenged.

Furthermore, rituals can be a source of comfort and solace. They provide us with a sense of familiarity and predictability, which can be especially important during times of uncertainty or change. By engaging in rituals, we tap into a deeper sense of connection to ourselves, our communities, and the world around us. This sense of connection can foster a greater sense of meaning and purpose in our lives, leading to increased well-being and fulfillment.

The creation of rituals is a deeply personal process. There is no one-size-fits-all approach, as the most effective rituals are those that align with our individual values, goals, and lifestyles. Some people may find solace in a morning ritual that involves meditation, yoga, and journaling, while others may prefer an evening ritual that involves reading, spending time with loved ones, and winding down before bed. The key is to experiment and find what works best for you.

To create rituals that are both effective and sustainable, it is important to start small and build gradually. Rather than trying to overhaul your entire routine overnight, start by incorporating one or two small rituals into your day. Once these rituals become ingrained habits, you can gradually add more. It is also important to be flexible and adaptable, adjusting your rituals as your needs and circumstances change.

Rituals can be created for various aspects of our lives, from our morning routines to our work habits to our leisure activities. Some common examples of rituals include:

Morning rituals: These rituals can set the tone for the entire day, helping us to wake up feeling refreshed, energized, and focused. They can include activities such as meditation, exercise, journaling, reading, or enjoying a healthy breakfast.

Work rituals: These rituals can help us to create a productive and focused work environment. They can include setting specific work hours, taking regular breaks, minimizing distractions, or using time management techniques such as the Pomodoro Technique.

Evening rituals: These rituals can help us to wind down before bed, promote relaxation, and prepare for a restful sleep. They can include activities such as reading, taking a warm bath, listening to calming music, or spending time with loved ones.

Weekend rituals: These rituals can help us to disconnect from work and recharge our batteries. They can include activities such as spending time in nature, pursuing hobbies, or simply relaxing and enjoying leisure time.

By incorporating rituals into our daily lives, we can create a sense of order, purpose, and meaning. We can automate our decision-making processes, free up our mental energy, and cultivate a deeper sense of connection to ourselves and the world around us. Rituals are not merely tools for time management; they are pathways to a more mindful, intentional, and fulfilling life.

The creation of rituals is a lifelong journey of self-discovery and refinement. As we evolve and grow, so too will our rituals. By embracing the power of rituals, we can unlock the true potential of our time and create a life that is both productive and joyful.

ᎠᎠᎠ

Continuous improvement is the path to mastery in time alchemy. By embracing a growth mindset, seeking feedback, and experimenting with different approaches, you can refine your time management practices and achieve lasting results.

EIGHTEEN

THE 80/20 RULE: LEVERAGING THE POWER OF FOCUS

In the vast expanse of human endeavor, where countless tasks and responsibilities vie for our attention, the 80/20 Rule, also known as the Pareto Principle, emerges as a guiding light, illuminating a fundamental truth about the nature of cause and effect. This principle, named after the Italian economist Vilfredo Pareto, who first observed it in the distribution of wealth in the late 19th century, posits that roughly 80% of outcomes result from 20% of causes. While initially applied to economics, the 80/20 Rule has since been found to hold true in a wide range of domains, from business and productivity to personal relationships and health.

At its core, the 80/20 Rule is a principle of disproportionality, revealing that a small fraction of our efforts often yields the majority of our results. In the realm of time management and productivity, this principle suggests that a mere 20% of our tasks and activities are responsible for 80% of our achievements. By identifying and focusing on this vital few, we can leverage the power of focus to achieve exponential results, streamline our efforts, and create a life of greater impact and fulfillment.

The 80/20 Rule challenges the conventional wisdom that hard work alone is the key to success. While effort is undoubtedly important, the principle suggests that it is not the sheer quantity of our work that matters most, but rather the quality and strategic allocation of our efforts. By identifying the 20% of tasks that yield the greatest results and focusing our energy on these high-impact activities, we can achieve far more than we ever thought possible.

In the realm of business, the 80/20 Rule can be a game-changer. By identifying the 20% of customers who generate 80% of revenue, companies can tailor their marketing and sales efforts to better serve these high-value clients. This can lead to increased customer loyalty, higher profit margins, and a more sustainable business model. Similarly, by focusing on the 20% of products or services that generate the most revenue, businesses can streamline their offerings, reduce costs, and improve overall profitability.

The 80/20 Rule can also be applied to personal productivity. By identifying the 20% of tasks that contribute most to our goals, we can prioritize these activities and delegate or eliminate the rest. This can free up valuable time and energy for the things that truly matter, leading to increased focus, productivity, and overall satisfaction.

In the realm of personal relationships, the 80/20 Rule suggests that a small number of our relationships account for the majority of our happiness and fulfillment. By investing time and energy in cultivating these high-quality relationships, we can create a strong support network, enhance our well-being, and build lasting bonds that enrich our lives.

The 80/20 Rule can even be applied to our health and well-being. Research has shown that a small number of lifestyle factors, such as diet, exercise, and stress management, account for the majority of our health outcomes. By focusing on these key factors, we can improve our overall health, reduce our risk of chronic diseases, and live longer, healthier lives.

While the 80/20 Rule is a powerful tool for achieving success, it is important to remember that it is not a rigid formula. The exact ratio of 80/20 may not always hold true, and the specific tasks, activities, or factors that fall into the 20% category may vary depending on individual circumstances and goals. The key is to identify the patterns of disproportionality that exist in our lives and use this knowledge to make informed decisions about where to focus our time and energy.

Furthermore, the 80/20 Rule is not an excuse for neglecting the remaining 80% of tasks or activities. While it is important to prioritize the vital few, we must also acknowledge the importance of the trivial many. These tasks may not contribute significantly to our immediate goals, but they may still be necessary for maintaining our overall well-being, fostering creativity, or building relationships.

The 80/20 Rule is a guiding principle, not a rigid rule. It is a lens through which we can view the world, a framework for understanding the dynamics of cause and effect. By embracing this principle, we can learn to focus our efforts on the tasks and activities that truly matter, achieving greater results with less effort, and creating a life of greater impact and fulfillment. The 80/20 Rule is not a shortcut to success, but rather a roadmap for achieving our goals with greater efficiency, focus, and intentionality. It is a reminder that we are not limited by the constraints of time, but rather by the choices we make about how we use it.

ᘓᘓᘓ

The time alchemist's legacy is a life of purpose and fulfillment. By mastering the art of time management, you can create a life that is both meaningful and impactful, leaving a lasting legacy for generations to come.

NINETEEN

CONTINUOUS IMPROVEMENT: REFINING YOUR TIME ALCHEMY

The journey towards mastery in any discipline, be it art, music, sports, or time management, is a lifelong endeavor. It is a continuous process of learning, growth, and refinement, where we strive to expand our knowledge, hone our skills, and push the boundaries of our potential. Time alchemy, the art of transforming our relationship with time to achieve greater productivity, fulfillment, and well-being, is no exception. As we embark on this transformative journey, we must embrace the principle of continuous improvement, recognizing that mastery is not a destination, but an ongoing process of refinement and evolution.

Continuous improvement is a philosophy that permeates every aspect of our lives. It is the relentless pursuit of excellence, the unwavering commitment to learning and growing, and the constant striving to become the best version of ourselves. In the realm of time alchemy, continuous improvement is the key to unlocking our full potential, to refining our time management practices, and to achieving lasting and meaningful results.

The first step in embracing continuous improvement is to cultivate a growth mindset. This is a belief that our abilities and intelligence can be developed through dedication and hard work. It is a rejection of the fixed mindset, which views our abilities as static and unchangeable. With a growth mindset, we embrace challenges, persist in the face of setbacks, and view failures as opportunities for learning and growth.

In the context of time alchemy, a growth mindset empowers us to experiment with different techniques, adapt to changing circumstances, and continually refine our time management practices. It encourages us to step outside our comfort zones, to try new approaches, and to learn from our successes and failures. By embracing a growth mindset, we open ourselves up to a world of possibilities, where growth and improvement are not only possible but inevitable.

Another essential component of continuous improvement is self-reflection. This involves taking a step back and examining our time management practices with a critical eye. We ask ourselves questions such as: "What is working well? What could be improved? What am I learning from my successes and failures?" By reflecting on our experiences, we gain valuable insights into our strengths, weaknesses, and areas for growth.

Self-reflection can take many forms, such as journaling, meditation, or simply taking a few moments each day to pause and reflect on our time usage. It is important to approach self-reflection with an open mind and a willingness to learn. By identifying areas where we can improve, we can make adjustments to our time management practices and continue our journey towards mastery.

Feedback is another invaluable tool for continuous improvement. By seeking feedback from others, we can gain valuable insights into our blind spots, our strengths, and our areas for growth. Feedback can come from a variety of sources, such as colleagues, mentors, coaches, or even friends and family.

When seeking feedback, it is important to be open and receptive to constructive criticism. We must be willing to acknowledge our shortcomings and take steps to address them. Feedback is not a personal attack, but rather an opportunity for growth and development. By incorporating feedback into our time management practices, we can continuously refine our approach and achieve greater results.

Experimentation is another key element of continuous improvement. In the realm of time alchemy, there is no one-size-fits-all solution. What works for one person may not work for another. Therefore, it is essential to experiment with different techniques and approaches to find what works best for us.

This may involve trying out different time management tools, such as calendar apps, task management software, or time tracking apps. It may also involve experimenting with different scheduling techniques, such as time blocking, batching tasks, or the Pomodoro Technique. By experimenting with different approaches, we can discover the strategies that best suit our individual needs and preferences.

In addition to experimentation, continuous improvement also involves learning from the successes and failures of others. By studying the time management practices of successful individuals, we can gain valuable insights and inspiration. We can also learn from the mistakes of others, avoiding pitfalls and identifying potential solutions to common challenges.

Continuous improvement is not a linear process. It is a cyclical journey of learning, growth, and refinement. We may encounter setbacks and obstacles along the way, but by embracing a growth mindset, seeking feedback, experimenting with different approaches, and learning from others, we can continuously refine our time alchemy and achieve greater mastery over our time.

The pursuit of continuous improvement is not just about achieving greater productivity or efficiency. It is about cultivating a lifelong love of learning, a passion for growth, and a commitment to becoming the best version of ourselves. By embracing this philosophy, we can transform our relationship with time from one of scarcity and stress to one of abundance and fulfillment. We can unlock our full potential, achieve our goals, and create a life that is both meaningful and impactful.

In the grand tapestry of life, time is the most precious thread, and continuous improvement is the loom that allows us to weave a masterpiece of accomplishment. By embracing the principles of continuous improvement, we can refine our time alchemy, transform our lives, and create a legacy that will endure long after we are gone.

ΦΦΦ

Time is not just a resource; it is the canvas upon which you paint the masterpiece of your life. Embrace the power of time alchemy and create a life that is both extraordinary and fulfilling.

TWENTY

THE TIME ALCHEMIST'S LEGACY: LIVING A LIFE OF PURPOSE AND FULFILLMENT

In the grand tapestry of existence, time is the most precious thread, weaving together the moments, days, and years that shape our lives. The Time Alchemist, the master of time management, understands that time is not merely a resource to be managed, but a gift to be cherished and utilized to its fullest potential. The legacy of the Time Alchemist is not measured in hours saved or tasks completed, but in the profound impact they have on their own lives and the lives of others. It is a legacy of purpose, fulfillment, and a life well-lived.

The Time Alchemist's journey is not simply about maximizing productivity or squeezing every last drop of efficiency from their day. It is a transformative process of self-discovery, where they uncover their passions, values, and aspirations, and align their actions with their deepest intentions. The Time Alchemist understands that time management is not about controlling time, but about mastering oneself, cultivating self-discipline, and making conscious choices that lead to a life of meaning and purpose.

At the heart of the Time Alchemist's legacy is the recognition that time is a finite resource. We are not granted an infinite number of hours, days, or years on this planet. This realization imbues the Time Alchemist with a profound sense of urgency and purpose, a desire to make the most of every moment, to live each day as if it were their last.

This sense of urgency does not lead to a frantic rush to cram as much as possible into each day. Rather, it inspires the Time Alchemist to prioritize their time with intentionality, to focus on the activities that truly matter, and to let go of the distractions and obligations that drain their energy and detract from their well-being.

The Time Alchemist understands that true fulfillment comes not from accumulating wealth, possessions, or achievements, but from living a life that is aligned with their values and purpose. They seek to make a positive impact on the world, to contribute their unique gifts and talents to something larger than themselves. This could involve pursuing a meaningful career, volunteering their time to a worthy cause, or simply being a loving and supportive presence in the lives of their family and friends.

The Time Alchemist's legacy is also characterized by a deep sense of gratitude. They recognize that time is a precious gift, not to be taken for granted. They cultivate an attitude of appreciation for each moment, savoring the simple joys of life, and finding beauty in the everyday. This gratitude extends to the people in their lives, as the Time Alchemist recognizes the importance of connection and community in creating a fulfilling life.

To cultivate a life of purpose and fulfillment, the Time Alchemist employs a variety of strategies and techniques. They set clear and compelling goals, create detailed plans, and prioritize their tasks with unwavering focus. They understand the importance of self-care, taking time to rest, recharge, and nurture their physical, mental, and emotional well-being. They also cultivate healthy habits and routines, automating their decision-making processes and freeing up their mental energy for more creative and fulfilling pursuits.

The Time Alchemist is not afraid to experiment and try new things. They recognize that the journey towards mastery is a continuous process of learning and growth. They embrace challenges as opportunities to expand their horizons, to learn new skills, and to discover hidden talents. They are constantly refining their time management practices, seeking out new tools and techniques, and adapting their approach to meet the ever-changing demands of life.

The Time Alchemist also understands the importance of balance. They recognize that a fulfilling life encompasses more than just work and productivity. They prioritize their relationships, their passions, and their well-being, ensuring that they are not neglecting any aspect of their lives in their pursuit of success. By cultivating a healthy balance between work, play, and rest, the Time Alchemist creates a sustainable and fulfilling lifestyle that supports their long-term goals and aspirations.

The legacy of the Time Alchemist is not confined to their own life. It ripples outward, touching the lives of those around them. The Time Alchemist inspires others through their example, demonstrating that it is possible to live a life of purpose, fulfillment, and impact. They mentor and guide others on their own journeys, sharing their wisdom, knowledge, and experience.

The Time Alchemist's legacy is also manifested in the tangible contributions they make to the world. Whether it is through their work, their creative endeavors, or their philanthropic efforts, the Time Alchemist leaves a lasting mark on the world, a testament to their commitment to making a difference.

In the end, the Time Alchemist's legacy is not about how much they accomplished, but about how they lived. It is about the quality of their relationships, the depth of their experiences, and the impact they had on the world. It is a legacy of purpose, passion, and a life well-lived.

The Time Alchemist's journey is not an easy one. It requires discipline, dedication, and a willingness to confront our own limitations and fears. But the rewards are immeasurable. By embracing the principles of time alchemy, we can unlock our full potential, create a life of meaning and purpose, and leave a lasting legacy that will inspire generations to come.

ᐅᐅᐅ

The present moment is a gift, not a burden. By embracing the power of now, you can unlock your full potential and create a life of abundance, joy, and lasting impact.

TWENTY-ONE
SUMMARY

The Time Alchemist: A Summary of Mastering Time Management for Peak Performance

Time, an elusive and precious resource, holds immense power in shaping our lives and achieving our goals. This book, "The Time Alchemist: Mastering Time Management for Peak Performance," serves as a comprehensive guide to understanding and harnessing the transformative power of time. Through a series of interconnected chapters, we have explored the intricacies of time management, delving into its psychological, practical, and philosophical dimensions.

The journey began by unmasking the illusion of time scarcity, a pervasive misconception that can lead to stress, anxiety, and overwhelm. We discovered that time is not a finite resource, but rather a subjective experience shaped by our perceptions, priorities, and choices. By cultivating mindfulness and focusing on the present moment, we can transcend the illusion of scarcity and tap into the abundance of time that lies within us.

We then delved into the fundamentals of time alchemy, the art of transforming our relationship with time to achieve greater productivity, fulfillment, and well-being. This involved developing awareness of our time usage patterns, identifying and eliminating time leaks, setting clear intentions, and embracing flexibility and mindfulness in our approach to time management.

The importance of goal setting as a compass for time navigation was also highlighted. By setting clear, specific, measurable, achievable, relevant, and time-bound (SMART) goals, we create a roadmap for our lives, ensuring that our actions are aligned with our desired outcomes. We learned that goal setting is an iterative process that requires ongoing reflection, adjustment, and course correction as we encounter challenges and obstacles along the way.

Prioritization emerged as a critical skill for navigating the complexities of modern life. By discerning the essential from the trivial and focusing our efforts on the tasks that truly matter, we can maximize our impact and achieve our goals more efficiently. We explored various prioritization frameworks, such as the Eisenhower Matrix, which helps us categorize tasks based on their urgency and importance, allowing us to make informed decisions about how to allocate our time and energy.

The power of time blocking, a technique that involves dividing our day into distinct blocks of time dedicated to specific tasks or activities, was also highlighted. By creating a personalized time blueprint, we can reduce distractions, increase focus, and achieve a state of flow, where we are fully immersed in our work and able to achieve optimal performance.

We delved into the Pomodoro Technique, a time management method that breaks down work into intervals separated by short breaks. This technique helps to overcome procrastination, promote deep work, and improve time management skills by providing a structured framework for our work.

We also explored the importance of overcoming procrastination, the insidious thief of time that can derail our productivity and leave us feeling frustrated and unaccomplished. By understanding the roots of procrastination, recognizing our triggers, and implementing effective strategies, we can break free from its grasp and reclaim our time, our productivity, and our peace of mind.

The power of batching tasks, or grouping similar activities together, was also highlighted as a means of increasing efficiency and productivity. By minimizing context switching and focusing on one type of task at a time, we can streamline our workflow, reduce mental fatigue, and achieve greater results in less time.

We discussed the importance of delegation as a multiplier of time, allowing us to leverage the talents and expertise of others to achieve outcomes that would be impossible alone. Effective delegation involves identifying tasks suitable for delegation, selecting the right individuals, providing clear communication and support, and offering regular feedback.

The power of saying "no" as a means of protecting our precious time was also emphasized. By learning to decline requests and opportunities that do not align with our values, goals, and priorities, we can reclaim our autonomy and create space for the things that truly matter.

We explored the concept of mindful time management, the art of integrating mindfulness practices into our daily routines to harness the power of the present moment. By cultivating present moment awareness, non-judgmental acceptance, clear intentions, healthy boundaries, and gratitude, we can transform our relationship with time and create a life that is more balanced, fulfilling, and purposeful.

The role of digital tools as allies in our time management journey was also discussed. From calendar apps to task management software to time tracking tools, these digital companions can help us to organize our tasks, schedule our time, and gain valuable insights into our productivity patterns.

We also delved into the importance of energy management, recognizing that energy, not time, is the fundamental currency of our lives. By prioritizing nutrition, sleep, exercise, and stress management, we can cultivate a strong and resilient physical, mental, and emotional energy that fuels our productivity and well-being.

The significance of rest and relaxation was highlighted as essential components of a balanced and productive life. By allowing our bodies and minds to recharge, we can prevent burnout, enhance creativity, and achieve greater long-term success.

The creation of rituals, intentional and repetitive actions that we incorporate into our daily routines, was presented as a powerful tool for time management on autopilot. By automating our decision-making processes and creating a sense of structure and stability, rituals can help us to maximize our productivity and achieve our goals with greater ease and efficiency.

Finally, we explored the 80/20 Rule, a principle of disproportionality that reveals that a small fraction of our efforts often yields the majority of our results. By identifying and focusing on the 20% of tasks that contribute most to our goals, we can leverage the power of focus to achieve exponential results and create a life of greater impact and fulfillment.

In conclusion, "The Time Alchemist" offers a comprehensive and insightful guide to mastering time management for peak performance. By embracing the principles and strategies outlined in this book, we can transform our relationship with time, reclaim control of our schedules, and create a life that is both productive and fulfilling. The journey towards mastery is a continuous one, requiring ongoing learning, growth, and refinement. However, by embracing the principles of continuous improvement, we can refine our time alchemy skills, achieve our goals, and leave a lasting legacy of purpose and fulfillment.

ᚦᚦᚦ

Citation And References

This book represents the culmination of extensive research and meticulous analysis, incorporating a diverse range of sources, including numerous books, scholarly studies, and personal experiences. Additionally, I have scoured various websites to gather relevant information and data essential for the compilation of this work. I have taken every precaution to ensure the accuracy of the information presented and have diligently cited all sources to acknowledge their contributions.

Despite these efforts, the possibility of inadvertent errors remains. I deeply value the insights of my readers and appreciate any feedback that can help identify and rectify such inaccuracies. I encourage you to bring any discrepancies to my attention.

Your feedback is not only welcome but crucial, as it will aid in correcting current editions and enhancing the content of future ones. I am committed to maintaining the highest standards of accuracy and reliability in my work and thank you for your support and understanding.

Additionally, I firmly uphold the principle of freedom of speech and expression as guaranteed under Article 19(1)(a) of the Constitution of India, and I respect the diverse viewpoints and expressions of all readers.

🙏🙏🙏

Other Books Of The Author

1. Empowering Minds: A Journey into Women's Self-Discovery and Power
2. The Dynamics of Motivation: Catalyzing Thought into Action
3. Meditation and Mental Well Being: The Path to Inner Peace and Clarity
4. The Psychology of Child Education: Nurturing Future Generations
5. Ethical Enlightenment: A Modern Guide to Living with Integrity
6. Voices of Empowerment: Stories of Women Rising Against Odds
7. Social Psychology in Everyday Life: Understanding Human Connections
8. The Essence of Motivational Speaking: Inspiring Change in Others
9. Balancing Acts: Women, Work, and the Will to Lead
10. Guiding with Grace: Raising Children with Compassion and Awareness
11. The Power of Positive Aging: Embracing Life After Fifty
12. Building Resilient Communities: Social Work in Action
13. The Ethical Educator: Principles for Teaching and Learning
14. From Insight to Impact: Social Psychology for a Better World
15. The Ethics of Empathy: A Guide to Ethical Living
16. The Science of Empowering the Self: Navigating Life's Challenges with Psychological Wisdom
17. The Mindful Conscious Leader: Meditation Techniques for Modern Management
18. Pioneering Spirit: Women's Pathways to Leadership and Empowerment
19. Feeling to Healing: The Role of Emotional Intelligence in Child Development
20. Transformative Talks and Words of Inspiration: Insights into Motivational Oratory

in a Complex World

46. Secret of Solopreneur's Odyssey: Navigating the Path to Self-Employment
47. Exploring Tapestry of Peace: Global Perspectives on Harmony
48. The Art and Actions of Connection: Mastering Communication for Impact
49. She Governs and at the Helm: Strategies for Political Empowerment
50. Rising Above and Rising with Grace: A Woman's Roadmap to Career Mastery
51. The Effect of Networking & Connectedness: Building Strategic Alliances for Women
52. Beyond his Barriers: Women Thriving in Male-Dominated Fields
53. Secret of Inner Compass: Navigating Life with Intuition
54. Creative & Pro-Active Muses: A Celebration of Women in the Arts
55. Unburdened: The Art of Releasing the Past
56. Amplified Voices: Speeches of Women that Astonished the World
57. Secret of Manifesting Dreams: A Woman's Guide to Intentional Living
58. Ethics and Value Based Education: Reimagining Japan's School System
59. The Moral Compass Curriculum: A Holistic Approach
60. Tech with Heart: Integrating Ethics into Digital Learning
61. Honoring Virtue: Recognizing Ethical Excellence in Education
62. Raising Good Humans: A Guide to Character Development
63. The Spark Within: Nurturing Creativity in Children
64. The Teenager Whisperer: Navigating Adolescence with Grace
65. Igniting a Passion for Learning: Inspiring Lifelong Curiosity
66. The Habit Lab: Cultivating Positive Behaviors in Children
67. Seeds of Empathy: Fostering Compassion in Young Hearts
68. The Reading Revolution: Inspiring a Love of Books in Children
69. The Learning Brain: Unlocking the Secrets of Student Success
70. Teaching for All: Differentiated Instruction Strategies
71. The Time Alchemist: Mastering Time Management for Peak Performance

72. The Resilience Factor: Transforming Setbacks into Stepping Stones
73. The Healing Touch of Nature: An Introduction to Naturopathy
74. Echoes of the Past: Healing Through Past Life Regression
75. The Spiritual Healer's Handbook: Exploring Energy Medicine
76. Crystal Clarity: Unveiling the Power of Gemstones
77. The Dream Weaver's Guide: Decoding the Language of Dreams
78. Emotional Alchemy: Transforming Pain into Power
79. Sonic Serenity: Harnessing Sound for Stress Relief
80. The Entrepreneur's Playbook: Launching Your Business with Confidence
81. Productivity Unleashed: Time Management Strategies for Entrepreneurs
82. The Problem Solver's Toolkit: Creative Solutions for Business Challenges
83. The Future is Now: Emerging Trends in Business
84. The Curious Explorer: A Child's Guide to Scientific Discovery
85. Digital Pioneers: Empowering Kids in the Tech World
86. The Young Philosopher's Guide: Exploring Life's Big Questions
87. Finding Your Voice: Communication Skills for Confident Kids
88. Nature's Playground: A Child's Guide to Outdoor Adventure
89. Growing a Greener Tomorrow: A Guide to Tree Planting & Conservation
90. Driving with Purpose: Ethical Choices on the Road
91. The Healing Touch: Cultivating Compassion in Healthcare
92. Navigating the Digital Landscape: Ethics in the Age of Social Media
93. The Ethical Closet: A Guide to Sustainable Fashion
94. The Mindful Voyager: Sustainable Travel Practices
95. The Feminine Divine: Honoring the Goddesses of India
96. Sacred Sounds: Chanting Your Way to Inner Peace
97. The Yoga Path: Uniting with the Divine Within
98. Rites of Passage: Creating Meaningful Ceremonies
99. The Chakra System: A Map of Inner Transformation
100. Spiritual Sangha: Finding Community through Satsang and

Bhajan

101. Pilgrimage of the Soul: Spiritual Journeys in India

❧❧❧

Contact

Dr. Minakshi Bansal
Social Activist
Ahmedabad, Gujarat, Bharat
minakshiindiag20@yahoo.com

❦❦❦

|| LOKAHA SAMASTHAHA SUKHINO BHAVANTU ||